FINDING
ENLIGHTENMENT

FINDING
ENLIGHTENMENT

Ramtha's School of Ancient Wisdom

J. Gordon Melton

BEYOND
WORDS
Publishing
I   N   C

Beyond Words Publishing, Inc.
20827 N.W. Cornell Road, Suite 500
Hillsboro, Oregon 97124-9808
503-531-8700
1-800-284-9673

C&E™, Consciousness & Energy™, Fieldwork™, The Tank™, Blue Body Healing™, Blue Body Dance™, and Twilight Visualization Process™ are trademarks of JZ Knight, d/b/a/ JZK, Inc., a Washington corporation, and are used with permission. Permission from JZK, Inc., is gratefully acknowledged for inclusion herein of drawings by Don Marshall entitled "Binary Thinking" (page 106) and "Analogical Thinking" (page 107).

Editor: Sue Mann
Cover design: Jennifer Viviano
Interior design, graphics (pp. 88, 96, 99, 106, 107), and composition: Rohani
    Design, Edmonds, Washington
Proofreader: Marvin Moore

Printed in the United States of America
Distributed to the book trade by Publishers Group West

Library of Congress Cataloging-in-Publication Data

Melton, J. Gordon.
    Finding enlightenment : Ramtha's school of ancient wisdom /
J. Gordon Melton.
        p.   cm.
    Includes bibliographical references.
    ISBN 978-1-4516-8785-9
    1. Ramtha's School of Enlightenment. 2. Ramtha, the
enlightened one (Spirit) 3. Knight, J. Z. (Judy Zebra), 1946–   .
4. Gnosticism—Miscellanea. I. Title.
BP605.R37M45 1997
299'.93—dc21   97-21810
                                                CIP

The corporate mission of Beyond Words Publishing, Inc.:
Inspire to Integrity

To

Audrey, Brett, Debbie, Diane, Don, Gary,

Greg, J.O., Joe, Melissa, Michele, Michelle,

Molly, Nancy, Pevel, Suzie, Vicki, and Zafi.

Thanks for all your help.

CONTENTS

INTRODUCTION

I stood in the back of the large auditorium as lively music played. A thousand people packed the room, many standing and swaying with the music. Then, all of a sudden from one end of the space whoops and hollers went up, and within a second the whole audience joined in. You would have thought a celebrity, like Madonna or Willie Nelson, had entered. In fact, that is what happened, for the woman who appeared was more important than a mere Mick Jagger or Neil Diamond, because she brought their teacher, Ramtha, whom they had come to hear.

The woman, JZ Knight, had pulled her hair into a ponytail and had dressed in a loose-fitting full-length tunic and boots. JZ,* having turned over her body to Ramtha, a noncorporeal entity, proceeded to the sound booth near where I stood. He—and it is now easier to think of the entranced JZ as he—greeted Debbie, the sound engineer, who attached the portable mike. He then turned to greet J. O. Ault, a student who had agreed to assist me and answer questions for the day. He then turned to greet me. As with J.O., he took my hands, kissed both front and back, and then leaned over

---

*In this book I refer to Knight as JZ to retain name consistency throughout her adult life.

and kissed my forehead. "Greetings, scribe!" he said. "Good morning, and thank you for allowing me to attend the school," I replied. Ramtha smiled knowingly and proceeded to the stage.

Ramtha then went through a ritual I was to see many times. He saluted the audience, "Indeed!" They roared back, "Indeed!" Holding up a cup, he said, "Let's have a drink of water." With their right hands they picked up water bottles and held them aloft. As Ramtha spoke each line, the audience repeated it:

> O my beloved God,
> Mysterious one,
> Of that which You are,
> I desire to know;
> Of that which I am,
> I desire to understand;
> Bless my life
> This fine day;
> Open my heart,
> And open my mind,
> That the mystery that is I,
> I may understand
> God help me so!
>
> So be It!
>
> To Life!

At the time I first heard those words, I hardly understood what they meant; when I could understand them, I had, indeed, learned a great deal.

MY PILGRIMAGE TO RAMTHA

In 1992, I was called to Ramtha's School of Enlightenment in Yelm, Washington, by JZ's lawyer to consult with him on a court proceeding. JZ's ex-husband was asking the court to reconsider their divorce settlement on the grounds that he had been coerced by cultic brainwashing into settling for far less than the family estate would dictate. After the trial was over, I asked JZ if she would allow me to write a book about her and the school. If what I had seen and heard was a representative sample of the school's curriculum, then she had developed a noteworthy religious community and I wanted to be the one to document it. She said she would think about it. I went back to Santa Barbara and immersed myself in vampires, the Branch Davidian siege in Waco, and a research project on religious pluralism in Los Angeles. I assumed she had decided against the book, and I had plenty to keep me busy.

Then one evening many months later, as I was eating supper JZ phoned. She said that after the trial she had in fact tabled my proposal but had recently reconsidered and was ready to go ahead with it. Was I still interested? I was interested enough to set a time for an initial visit (February 1994) before we got off the phone.

Thus it was a few weeks later that I found myself back in Yelm laying out a program for the study. JZ agreed to all my terms. I would go through the year of basic classes as if I were a beginning student. I would have complete and free access to talk to all the students, and I could pass out questionnaires at the events. Although the school had no written curriculum, audiotapes had been made of all the classes and special events, and I could obtain copies of any tapes I deemed pertinent, especially those of classes and events I had attended. JZ also promised to give of her time amid a busy schedule that included both channeling Ramtha and serving as the school's chief executive officer.

Over the next two years I went to Yelm every time I could break away from an otherwise full schedule. I was eventually able to attend all levels of classes and occasionally sit in on special events. Occasionally, JZ invited me to stay at her home while attending events; thus, I had the opportunity to see her household, visit informally with her and (important for me) her household staff, and observe her before and after Ramtha entered her body. As my study began to take shape and as I shared with her some observations of the school, I also suggested that other scholars would jump at the opportunity to have an opportunity similar to mine. After considering that suggestion for some months, she allowed me to invite about a dozen colleagues to the school. Eventually, their visit resulted in a conference held in Yelm in February 1997. Although the main body of material coming out of that conference will be published in a subsequent volume, I integrated a few of the more important findings into this text.

RESULTS OF A STUDY

I wanted to accomplish several distinct tasks in this book. First and foremost, much as an anthropologist approaching a newly discovered people, I have tried to summarize and chronicle the history, worldview, leadership, and practices of Ramtha's School of Enlightenment. I have acted somewhat as a church historian (a decidedly unpopular occupation these days) and discuss the life of the founder and the history of the institution she founded much as if it were a new religious body. I have written as if the school were a substantive and discrete social entity in a world of similar entities, a means of constructing reality certainly open for debate. However, it is one that has served me well in organizing a large body of data for analysis.

I begin with a straightforward account of JZ's origin, from her birth in rural New Mexico to the launching of her career as a channel. Then I switch to Ramtha and his life 35,000 years ago, when, he claims, he was a warrior and conqueror.

In chapter 3, I turn to a discussion of Gnosticism. Gnostic wisdom suggests that humans are, in fact, angelic, even divine, beings who have been lost in a world of distractions and forgetfulness, limitation and lack, public opinion and confining traditions. It poses the question, "What would it be like if you could actually remember your divine station, comprehend the potentials you possess, and manifest those potentials?"

Like most leaders of and adherents to metaphysical and esoteric organizations, I found JZ and her associates mostly unaware of the background of the ideas upon which they were drawing. During the 1990s JZ had become interested in Ramtha's intellectual roots and had discovered the likeness of Ramtha's teachings to alchemy, speculative Masonry, and Rosicrucianism. She had even selected books on these topics for the school's bookstore. However, while attending the school's beginning weekend event, I casually mentioned that Ramtha had laid out what resembled a classic ancient Gnostic system. The remark immediately caught JZ's attention, and she began to ask questions. To my subsequent minilecture on the Western Gnostic tradition, she responded, "So that's who we are?" I was frankly impressed that she showed interest, because most esotericists are completely alienated from history. I was unaware that at the time she was reworking the school's publicity material and that our conversation not only had spoken to her intellectual thirst but also had assisted her in solving a minor identity problem.

Chapter 4 discusses the beginning of the Knight/Ramtha phenomenon as well as channeling in general within the context of the New Age. Chapters 5 and 6 form the heart of this book. The former discusses Ramtha's Gnostic philosophy—the underpinnings of his school—and the latter, the spiritual practices that put his philosophy to work.

During the school's ten-year period, a religious community tied together by the acceptance of Ramtha's teachings has emerged. The student body has proved to be almost as interesting as the teacher who brought it together. Students form a distinctive subculture in the larger New Age community. They have founded their own variation on popular New Age ideas and, more important for the long-term health of the community, have created a rich cultural life. Student life is explored in chapter 7.

Finally, the school has reached its tenth anniversary in spite of a variety of obstacles. JZ and Ramtha have been the subjects of intense controversy. That controversy first brought me into contact with the school, and throughout the study I continually encountered Ramtha's critics. Psychic skeptics reduced any claims of contact between humans and spirit entities to imaginary or pathological activities of the person making such contact, no matter how extraordinary the contact might be. Other harsher critics, including some former students, claimed that Ramtha is simply a fraud and JZ is, in fact, the center of an elaborate and profitable hoax. The accusation of fraud appeals to reporters (it makes good copy) and to lawyers (it suggests legal responsibility), and it has often been repeated in the media coverage of the movement that has grown around Ramtha. Although outside the main thrust of my research, the controversy inevitably intruded and I knew that in the end I would have to reach an assessment of the many accusations leveled against the school, Ramtha, and JZ. Chapter 8 is devoted to a consideration of such issues.

This volume is the first systematic summary of the philosophy, activity, and world of Ramtha and his students. For that reason, and because of the multitudinous sources of information I consulted, I have talked with JZ throughout the process of writing, double-checking that I have correctly understood the teachings. Then, I have tried to put what I understood in my own words and to avoid as much as possible Ramtha's words. At the same time, I will be rewarded if Ramtha's students recognize in my words an acceptable presentation of their beliefs and practices.

A NOTE ON THE NEW AGE AND OCCULTISM

JZ has rightly been seen as an integral part of the larger phenomenon called the New Age movement, although she separated herself from it soon after she started channeling publicly. The New Age movement originated in England in the 1960s by a variety of spiritual and esoteric groups that believed the end of the twentieth century would mark a transition point in history. New cosmic forces were being made available to humankind that would, over a generation, lead to a new era of peace, justice, and light. That vision was spread across Europe and was brought to North America in the 1970s. Throughout the 1980s the spiritual and metaphysical community in the United States grew tremendously because of that vision.

The essence of the New Age message was the promise of personal transformation. It would come in many forms, including physical healing, resolution of conflicts, and spiritual enlightenment. It would begin in small steps and became a continuous process with new realizations possible throughout life. The experience of individual transformation would become the hope of societal transformation. Social groups could be healed, nations could resolve conflicts, and the world could be reorganized with an enlightened structure.

Even as the New Age movement grew through the 1960s, it ran into conflict. Critics charged it with naiveté and journalists ridiculed its attachment to crystals and channeling. During the late 1980s its leaders carried on an intensive debate about the future of the movement, and by the end of the decade many, including such prominent figures as Jeremy Tarcher and David Spangler, abandoned the vision. They concluded, for whatever reason, that society was not moving toward the predicted change. What was real, however, was the personal transformation many members of the movement were experiencing.

Slowly, through the early 1990s, people began to realize that the movement was dying, and fewer and fewer designated themselves as New Agers. But the several million people changed by the movement did not go away; they did not return to the mundane existence of previous years. They just slowly adjusted to the ongoingness of life and transferred their emphases to personal quests for an expanded consciousness and an enlightened spirituality.

So what do we call this new phase of events? There is no real name, and so the name *New Age* has hung on even though the hope of a new age has mostly passed from the scene. In this volume I occasionally use the terms *New Age* and *New Ager* to designate those who have experienced some transformation because of their contacts with metaphysical, esoteric, psychic, and other mystical teachings. In doing so, I had to settle for the closest label I know of for this large and diverse community.

The word *occult* is one of the more controversial terms used when discussing the realities of Spiritualism, Gnosticism, and spiritual metaphysics. The term has been somewhat degraded in popular parlance; many think of the occult as the most questionable aspects of the psychic world, such as fortune-telling and sinister secret societies. As used here, however, the occult simply refers to its original meaning, namely, that which is hidden and specifically those hidden realities open only to the inner psychic vision. Occultism, the philosophy derived from an encounter with the occult realm, formed the substance taught in the mystery schools of the ancient world. A working knowledge of the occult often follows the disciplined practice of psychic development, usually with the guidance of a master teacher.

J. Gordon Melton

JZ AND MEETING
THE ONE

S he was a young, successful businesswoman in Manhattan
Beach, California, who had no need for a fortune-teller.
However, JZ Hensley's friend wanted to visit one and she agreed to
go. As they entered the dimly lit rooms, the fortune-teller, an older
woman, focused her attention on JZ. JZ's friend said that she was
the one who had made the appointment. The fortune-teller smiled
at her, but just as swiftly turned her attention back to a somewhat
confused JZ and said, "I have been waiting for you." The friend
interrupted, "I think you have us mixed up. I am the one who made
the appointment." This time the fortune-teller merely ignored her
and said, indicating JZ, "I have been waiting for this one." She led
JZ into the room where she gave her readings.[1]

JZ tried to refocus the woman's attention. "I really don't want
to know anything. My friend needs to know . . ." The woman cut
her off, instructing her to make a fist and hold it above her head.
Then the woman took her hand, and JZ slowly opened her palm.
"I will first tell you something about your past," the woman said.
JZ had become just a distant observer. She was simply above it all,
at least for a few minutes.

JZ quickly lost her smugness as the woman said, "You are an
uncertain woman. You married a man you did not love. You had

two children from this marriage . . . two boys. You left the man. You are not from here. You are from where the coyotes howl. You are in television . . . communications . . . you market this . . . you are very good." The woman was correct. She now had JZ's complete attention.

"Now, I must tell you about your future." She paused only a second. "Very soon you will leave this place. You will go where it is hot . . . very hot. You will have fire on your back." At this negative prediction, JZ reacted. "You mean I will be in a wreck or something?"

"No," the woman assured her. "Only your back will burn. You will be in the place of heat for three weeks. Then you will have two offers of work. One will be where the sky is dark with business. The other will be a place with great mountains, tall pines, and lakes that shine like mirrors unto the heavens. If you go to the mountains and pines, you will meet The One. Do you understand?"

JZ replied honestly, "I don't understand any of what you said." But every word had become fixed in her memory.

"You will. . . . If you meet The One, you will have great influence . . . great destiny. I have waited for you. Now, I have told you. It is done." The trancelike expression the woman had held during the reading dissipated and her face relaxed.

Struck by the unfathomable reading, JZ retained enough presence to ask the woman's fee, but she refused any pay, merely remarking, "You owe only to yourself."

Later JZ and her friend talked about the reading. JZ wondered who The One could be—maybe the man she had hoped for when she had married.

The next day her boss called. Could she drop everything and move to Waco, Texas, to set up a cable TV system there? She accepted, and three days later she was off to "where it was hot." Unaware of what she was really doing, JZ began a journey that would lead her to Ramtha: The One. In the meantime, as a valued executive in an expanding business, she had already traveled far from the small New Mexico town where her present life had begun.

ORIGINS

The woman who now leads Ramtha's School of Enlightenment had, to say the least, an auspicious beginning. She was born Judith Darlene Hampton in Roswell, New Mexico, on March 16, 1946. She was named for Judith, the heroine of the Book of Judith.[2] The family lived in Dexter, New Mexico, not far from Roswell. Her mother, who kept the family together, would later tell her of a Yaqui Indian woman who held the two-week-old Judith and in her broken English said, "Helen, this li'l girl of yourn will see what no one else sees . . . her destiny . . . important."

Judith had three older brothers—Charles Jr., Gayle, and Donnie—and a sister, Wanda. She would later be joined by a younger brother, Loy Gene. Her father, Charles, was a tenant farmer, but he is more remembered for his alcohol abuse and absence from the family. Her mother divorced before Judith was school age and eventually married again. Her stepfather provided for her but was emotionally distant.

Judith's mother was not a churchgoer, but Judith's babysitters were both religious women and they took her to church. At least some teachings were absorbed, and through her preteen years, Judith began informally to teach the Bible to neighborhood children. On occasion she was not opposed to answering hostile comments about her lessons with her fists.

Judith's mother did not talk much about them, but she regularly had accurate precognitive dreams and often relied upon the information they supplied. JZ recounts the story of coming home one day from majorette tryouts at the local school. She found her room redone—a new bedspread, satin throws on the pillows, and new lace curtains. And possibly more important for a young teenager was a collection of cosmetics, her first. As Judith thanked her mother, her mother said, "Well, I tell ya, Judy, I knew you was a-goin' to make majorette cuz I dreamed it. My dreams always foretell me things. All my life they have. So, I saw ya marchin' round in this here dream."

3

At one point her mother confessed to knowing when family members were going to die because they would appear in her dreams. Not only did the dreams come true, but she had "suspicions" about things (a kind of clairvoyance) that, through common sense, she had learned to interpret accurately. At one point when the adult JZ was ill and in a hospital, her mother knew of her condition, quite apart from phone calls.

The most vivid experience for Judith during her growing-up years occurred one night at a friend's house. She and the other majorettes had gathered for a slumber party. Suddenly, about half past one in the morning, while looking out the window the girls saw blinding red flashes of light. Judith thought the end of the world had arrived. She remembered a prophecy in the Book of Revelation: that in the last days the moon would turn to blood and Jesus would return to rapture the saints to heaven. Then the flashes came directly through the window. The girls were now nearly hysterical, but before absolute panic set in, the lights disappeared. The girls returned to normal and went to bed. No more was said of the strange lights, and the next day no one remembered the incident.

Four years later Judith was a senior in high school and was talking with Kelly, who had hosted the slumber party. In the midst of the conversation, Judith's vision faded and inside her head she saw a flash of red light. Then she saw herself walking toward and into the light, blending with it. When her normal vision returned, she asked Kelly if she remembered the slumber party and the strange display of light. "Why had the girls never spoken of it?" she exclaimed. "It just doesn't make any sense that we didn't talk about something that weird. It's as if we weren't *supposed* to remember it."

The normally open Kelly refused to talk about the event and said, "Hampton, just drop it, OK?"

So Judith had a problem. What happened, and why couldn't anyone remember it? Had the girls made themselves forget it, or had some outside force been at work? She could not answer the question, but a conversation with her science teacher helped her tie it to UFOs and launch a lifelong interest in flying saucers.

A NEW DIRECTION

UFOs, suspicions, and precognitive dreams aside, Judith's life could have taken quite a different turn had it not been for two religious incidents. The first occurred in Sunday school. She was thirteen years old and she had some biblical questions. She began with one of the harder ones, the seeming contradiction between the two creation stories in the first chapters of Genesis. If that were not enough, she questioned the morals of a God who seemed to encourage Lot's rape of his own daughters, approve of Abraham's giving Sarah to other men to save his life, and justify Jacob's defrauding Esau of his birthright. If she had read the Bible correctly, these were serious moral lapses of the deity she was supposed to worship.

Of course there are answers to these questions; otherwise conservative biblical Christianity would have fallen under the onslaught of liberal Protestantism many decades ago. But the teacher had not yet been trained to answer them. Judith quickly took advantage of the situation to ask some equally troubling questions on the New Testament. The teacher, enraged, finally turned on Judith and attacked her faith.

A more crucial incident occurred later during a worship service. During the preacher's sermon, her half brother Marion and his wife, Tommy, walked into church and sat down. Marion had asked Tommy to wear lipstick, even though the church considered wearing makeup a sin. The minister saw Tommy and her reddened lips. He stopped his sermon and stared at her. He reminded everyone that wearing makeup was a sin that existed only as temptation for the flesh; that is, it would lead to illicit sex. He told her to join him in praying for God's forgiveness.

Judith watched as Tommy broke into tears. Slowly she rose and went to the altar rail. The minister began to pray for her

5

repentance. In the midst of this public reclaiming of the wandering soul, Marion simply walked out. Judith was incensed. God had approved of far worse actions by the Old Testament heroes. How could he condemn a little lipstick? The situation did not make sense. Judith stood up and shouted her disapproval. "I love my own good God. The God of my soul would not judge his own child like this." She drew an obvious conclusion. "I no longer belong here. It is finished." She walked out of the little church and turned her back on it and its teachings. She still clung to a faith in Jesus' message—that the kingdom of God was within and that to love all people would be to love God. If one accepted Jesus' message, she reasoned, being judgmental would be replaced with loving all people, never mind their beliefs or lack thereof. She would accept people just for who they are.

AN END TO ADOLESCENCE

6

Judith finished high school and looked forward to college. Her stepfather, however, had no money in his budget for female children to go to college. Her mother loaned her a small amount to see if she could work her way through. She moved to Lubbock and tried to survive at Texas Tech University. But the tuition was too high, and she settled for Lubbock Business College. She attended classes beginning at nine each morning. Additionally, she worked for several hours before classes and another few hours in the afternoons. Two evenings a week and all day Saturday and Sunday she filled in at the local supermarket. She found two roommates to share the rent. But the experiment did not work and she wound up in the hospital with a severe case of malnutrition. She moved home and abandoned her dream of a college education.

It was not long before Chris Hensley, a young man Judith had known in high school, came calling. She discovered they had some mutual interests, not the least being Judith's abilities with a rifle. She saw her relationship with Chris as making the most of a bad situation. They had been dating only a short time when they eloped to Mexico. Their first night as a married couple merely presaged what would become an increasingly unhappy relationship made tolerable by the birth of two children, Brandon and Christopher. Christopher was only a year old when the marriage fell apart because of Chris's alcohol abuse and infidelity. Judith left with the boys and began living with her mother in Hobbs, New Mexico. Judith soon settled in Roswell and became a salesperson for a new cable television company. The job would lead her to Manhattan Beach and her new name.

As Judith grew up she easily became Judy to her friends. But when she entered the business world she became Ms. Hensley. Somehow, neither name seemed right as she began to rise in the corporation. Her boss, Ben Mattson (who would also send her to Waco), raised the issue. He suggested that her image called for the formal *Mrs.* Hensley, yet her friendly, open style of leadership seemed to call for a less formal name, although not Judy. She noted that she had once been called Zebra because she frequently wore black and white. They played with the possibilities and came up with "JZ," no periods needed. It sounded right and it stuck.

THE PREDICTION STARTS

JZ and her sons moved to Waco, and she began the hard task of training a sales and maintenance force. Three weeks later she decided to take a day off. She spent the morning playing with her sons in the swimming pool at her apartment complex. In the afternoon, when the boys were napping, she returned to the pool for a sunbath and lay on her stomach. Her fatigue caught up with her and she fell asleep, only to awaken when the pain became too severe to ignore. In the bathroom mirror she saw a deep red glow emanating from her back. Chris awoke, saw her back, and asked, "Does it hurt, Mummy?" She replied, not considering her words, "Hurt? It's like my back is on fire." Only after she had spoken did she remember the fortune-teller's words.

She now had a valid excuse to spend a few more days at home. She was still recovering when her boss called to announce that the turnaround in Waco had occurred and that he wanted to send her to another area. She had two choices. As he began to tell her about them, she felt an eerie sensation—she knew what he would say. She could go to Bethlehem, Pennsylvania, or to Bremerton, Washington. The latter choice, near Seattle, was a beautiful location, according to Ben. "Lots of trees and mountains and lakes."

So far the fortune-teller was right: Bethlehem was a town "dark with business" (industrial pollution). As she made her choice to go to the Northwest, she said, "Ben, I must tell you that I am beginning to feel my life is being guided, somehow." Ben did not understand her, but he delivered a message from the person who had taken her to the fortune-teller. "Twila told me to tell you something about some old woman dying . . . and something about how she never found out anything. I hope you can figure that one out." JZ told him, "Please tell Twila that I think I'm going to meet The One."

Ben at least picked up on the strangeness of the message and bluntly told her, "You sound weird, JZ. We better get you the hell out of that place." She made one last try to explain what was happening. "I think I am destined to do something that makes a difference." He missed the point entirely. "Yeah, well you're already doing that, doll. Talk to you soon."

That call became a moment of change for JZ, a time of accepting a future that was rushing toward her. In the past God had used strange messengers to speak to his people, she knew. She offered a little prayer acknowledging the possibility that the fortune-teller had been guided to speak to her. "If so," she prayed, "then I accept the changes in my life and only pray that I will know the right thing to do. Father, grant me the wisdom I need to make the right moves and all the right decisions. I give great thanks to you for my life and the lives of my children."

A short time later, as JZ flew over the mountains into the Seattle-Tacoma Airport, the fortune-teller's words continued to

8

unfold. She saw the many lakes reflecting, just like mirrors, the light of the sun, and she saw the tall pines and great mountains. *If you go to the mountains and pines, you will meet The One.* And she had been living a long time as a single mother of two energetic boys.

She had settled in Tacoma for a year when, in the summer of 1973, the cable company, in spite of her success in the Puget Sound area, collapsed and she was suddenly without a job. However, with her self-confidence well established and with a good record in the business, she formed her own company, Mann Communications and Marketing, and was soon continuing her successful ways. It was not long before her staff realized that her success was not just from her executive skill and training abilities. Like her successful contemporaries, she integrated some psychic abilities into her decision making.[3] The staff began to talk about JZ working some "hocus-pocus." They were in awe of her knowing just where and when to send salespeople. Frank Smith, who recognized that his success had been markedly heightened by her decisions, confessed that he thought she was psychic. JZ was uncomfortable with the term, thinking that it took away from what she saw as the activity of God.

One day, Frank invited JZ to meet his aunt, whom he described as a kind of psychic. At first reluctant, JZ gave in when he added, "But she's says it's a gift from God." They arrived at Aunt Beau's in the afternoon. She was just rising from a nap and was still trying to wake, but she gave JZ a friendly hug, then suddenly stepped back, her hands trembling. She began to cry, though a smile graced her face.

Aunt Beau regained her composure quickly. She said, "Oh, my, now I understand. My dear child, you have the most awesome power walking with you."

"A power," JZ responded, "walking with me? What do you mean? I don't understand."

But Aunt Beau was becoming more enthusiastic. "I've never seen anything like it. . . . It's powerful . . . it's all around you. It's a blazing light, a powerful energy. I've seen energies, but never one like this."

JZ was just beginning to gain some sophistication about her abilities, but she didn't fully understand Aunt Beau's words. "Don't we all have some sort of light around us? Maybe even a guardian angel—it says that somewhere in the Bible."

"No," Aunt Beau cut her off, "not like this. This is timeless energy. It's just more than I can put into words. It's like a powerful god."

"What does that mean? You mean like God the Father?"

"No, it is *of* God. It is as if this power were life itself."

The conversation was reaching into the unknown and JZ's fear was building. "Is it an evil thing?"

Aunt Beau quickly calmed her. "Oh, no, no, no. It's the opposite. It's holy, child. This wonderful and holy light that walks with you will change many things in the world."

Fearful, but also fascinated, JZ asked, "But what is this thing that you say walks with me?"

Aunt Beau carefully chose her words. "I don't want to confuse you, and I don't want to sound blasphemous, but have you studied Jesus Christ and his teachings?" JZ nodded and Aunt Beau continued. "Well, dear child, it's a force on the same scale . . . a great teacher who will help engage the world in peace with his teaching."

Aunt Beau described the power as an immensely powerful masculine energy. As to how he would accomplish his mission, she could not say. It was still a mystery. She could not see him, only feel his power. And the light coming from him (though neither Frank nor JZ saw anything out of the ordinary) was overwhelming.

JZ, already living with the fortune-teller's predictions, was overwhelmed by Aunt Beau's additional message: "Please take care of your own energy. You seem extremely run down. This power with you can be profoundly draining unless you are completely rested and peaceful in your life."

Two weeks later JZ was in the hospital, suffering from exhaustion. A virus was attacking her bone marrow and white blood cells; degenerative mononucleosis was the diagnosis. As her hospital stay continued, she lost weight and her complexion turned pale, but the low point came when her hair fell out, a reaction to the drugs she was taking. As her disease progressed, she went home to continue what had become a semi-invalid condition.

Several weeks later, Frank stopped by with his fiancée. They were going to a revival meeting being held by a healing evangelist and invited her to attend. She was not impressed and was not in the mood to be very polite. "It's crap! It's not about God! I'm not walking down any aisle so somebody can save me from the devil." All her memories of church, especially her sister-in-law's ordeal, were still vivid.

Frank persisted. "Never mind the church. Do it for me so I won't feel I haven't tried to help you." Reluctantly, she agreed to go.

11

AN EVENTFUL RETURN TO CHURCH

As they settled in the revival tent, JZ was flooded by her pains—the physical pain in her back and the emotional pain of the last time she had attended church, some twenty years earlier. The songs were the same; the words were the same; the whole atmosphere was the same.

Then the preacher called for people to come forward for healing prayer. Now it was she, not her sister-in-law Tommy, who was headed toward the minister. She listened as he denounced the devil and called for Satan to depart from each soul. Finally it was her turn. She had gone this far for Frank, but her friendship and respect for his feelings could go only so far. She summoned all her executive authority and spoke to the minister. "Before you begin with me, I want to tell you something. I love God more than you can conceive of and more than you can preach. I denounced Satan a long time ago because he doesn't exist. He never did. When you understand the love of God, there is no room for evil or sin. Now I am dying. When you lay your hands on me, you pray for one who loves God. Don't even mention the name of Satan. He has no place here. He never has."

As she spoke the preacher listened intently, and the noise level in the audience dropped, as did not a few mouths. Heeding JZ's concern, he prayed with equal intensity. "O God, our Father, look upon this child and lift her life so that she may be healed. Oh God! Oh, God!"

Then occurred one of those events almost everyone yearns to see. A sudden flash of blue light came from the top of the tent and struck JZ, blasting the preacher and a woman standing next to him to the ground. The congregation gasped and was silent. JZ closed her eyes, aware that God had heard the prayer.

It took a few moments for the others to recover. Some began to murmur reactions to what they had seen. Even those who expected healing as a normal part of their church life now had to grasp a new level of the miraculous. Finally, someone had the presence of mind to come to the woman's and the preacher's aid.

"Who are you?" the minister asked. JZ responded without hesitating, "One of God's own." By that time Frank and his fiancée had reached JZ. They had seen everything and described the streak of blue light JZ only felt when it had entered her head. Suddenly, JZ was feeling wonderful. She was pain-free for the first time in many weeks, and a warm, light feeling pervaded her entire body. She was euphoric.

The dramatic healing (confirmed by medical tests over the next few days) gave JZ further theological insight. She had wondered why the godlike being or force who had attached itself to her would allow her to be ill. Now she understood that before she could be healed she had to cooperate with God. As she said, "I saved myself by trusting in God." Although she had been ready for God and his healing work, she was not prepared for the consequences of God working in her. She told Frank, "I might have been ready for God, but I wasn't ready for me. God needs

help, too. We are the only way God can express himself for us."
If you believe God and humans to be separate entities, rather
than God as an integral part of the true nature of each individual, she surmised, then it would be difficult to comprehend the
miracle that each person is. She felt she had a new understanding of God's plan.

MEETING THE ONE

During the next four years, which JZ described as uneventful, she
had time to become comfortable with her insights. Although she
had no connections to the larger metaphysical-psychic community, her experiences had led her into agreement with it. She had
developed a pantheistic, mystical view of the world, a view that
saw the world infused with God. She had come to feel that God
dwelled with her and that she had to love herself because she,
like each person, was, in her essential nature, identical with God.
She had become sick because she had thought too little of herself. She found herself agreeing with Aristotle's ideas of God
being the activity of the mind: "Pure self-activity of reason is
God's most blessed and everlasting life." She believed in reincarnation (and knew she had been her own sister, who had died
before she was born) and in UFOs.

13

And as her life progressed, she met Jeremy Wilder, a local
dentist. His beliefs were similar to hers, and they developed a
comfortable, loving relationship. He got along with her sons.
They married in 1977. No, Jeremy was not The One, but he was
the one who became the catalyst for JZ finally meeting The One.

The events began at a dinner party. JZ was attracted to a
comment she overheard about pyramid power. In the 1970s pyramids had become a great fad within the metaphysical-psychic
world. Several books, such as *Pyramid Power*, discussed the mysterious properties of properly aligned pyramids.[4] Pyramids would
preserve food. Dull razor blades placed within them would soon
become sharp. Some had suggested that pyramids actually accom-

plished the process of mummification. Pyramid tents appeared in which people meditated in the belief that psychic energy would be increased and their psychic powers would be heightened.

At the party JZ met George, who had placed a bottle of wine in a pyramid tent to see if the taste could be improved. George, a colleague of Jeremy's, was trying out some of the commonly suggested tests for the novice pyramid researcher. He had had great success and was enthusiastic about his findings and the ultimate possibilities of pyramids. JZ's interest was also aroused, and the next day she bought books on the subject. Jeremy made one pyramid and another and another, and by the next morning the house was full of pyramids, all properly aligned and housing a wide variety of fragrant objects, from a dirty tennis shoe to a banana. Jeremy's obsession threatened to overturn the natural order of things in their little home, and JZ reacted with anger and fear that the neighbors would discover what he was doing.

Jeremy continued through the day, and by Sunday morning even more pyramids graced various rooms. By early Sunday afternoon, JZ's anger gave way to humor and dedicated pyramid making gave way to a bout of hysterical laughter. JZ grabbed a paper pyramid reject, put it on her head, and in mock pomposity announced to her still-laughing husband, "Attention, attention please. You are now about to witness a miracle. We are about to place our new brain machine upon the willing victim, upon whom nature did not smile with great intelligence. Carefully we place the pyramid in the aligned position, encompassing the entire head and face. In moments, gentlemen, you will witness a truly magnificent transformation." They continued to laugh and share the hilarious climax of what had become a tension-filled weekend.

Then it happened. At first JZ saw a light at the other end of the kitchen, but her eyes were full of tears from laughing. When she wiped them away, there he was. She did not know it immediately, but he was The One, The One she had come to the Northwest to meet.

He was a giant of a man whose head touched the ceiling. Quite apart from his intimidating size, his appearance was unusual. He glowed with light, a dazzling display of purple. But his strange appearance calmed any fears of his being a simple intruder. His beautiful face attracted JZ, who was awestruck in his presence. A sense of peace filled the room. Only after she took in this amazing apparition did words begin to form.

"You are so beautiful. Who are you?"

"I am Ramtha, the Enlightened One. I have come to help you over the ditch."

Somehow, the word *ditch* did not seem to fit. What ditch? Is there a problem in the kitchen? Then the absurdity of the situation hit home, and JZ began to laugh again. She willed herself to wake up from what must be a dream. However, the "dream" continued, and the stranger spoke again. There was a lightness in his voice.

"Beloved woman, the greatest of things are achieved with a light heart. It is the ditch of limitation and fear I will help you over. For you will, indeed, beloved woman, become a light unto the world. Know that you are greatly loved, for the Father in heaven knows of you and loves you, greatly, indeed. Beloved woman, I desire you to know that you and your beloved family are in danger within this house. I desire you to be out of this place within five days in your counting and in number. Your children will dream a dream of that which is to come. Heed the dreams. Children are of the innocence to see many proud things, they are the prophets of a new age. I have prepared for you your new hovel. Indeed, there is a noble runner, entity, that will help you to find it. You will know who he is. Indeed, beloved woman, there are many changes coming. Prepare yourself. Know that you are greatly loved. I am Ramtha, the Enlightened One."

After speaking those words he disappeared, and JZ's kitchen returned to normal, though from that Sunday in February 1977 her life would never really return to normal again.

2

RAMTHA,
THE ONE

Who is Ramtha? According to his own account, Ramtha lived on Earth 35,000 years ago, in a time known today only through archeological remains and myths. He was a Lemurian, Lemuria forming the northern part of the ancient continent of Atlatia (Atlantis).[1] Its people concentrated on mind communication rather than on technology.

In contrast, the Atlanteans worshipped reason and progress, and through contact with extraterrestrials had even developed a flying machine. Atlantean science was even greater than that of the late twentieth century. Scientists had learned to "transform light into pure energy." However, because of their scientific experimentation, they caused a rip in the cloud cover that surrounded Earth, and a great deluge submerged the northern half of Atlantis, completely covering Lemuria.

The Lemurians fled south, and Ramtha's family began living in the slums of Onai, the great port city. However, by the time Ramtha was born Atlantis had lost its "scientific" leadership because of the destruction of its northern region. In the process, the southern lands lost not only their scientific gains and industry but also their more civilized social structure. The south fell into a feudal system whose tyrannical rulers pushed the refugee

Lemurians to the bottom of the social order. Ramtha graphically described his life: "Contemplate for a moment being spat upon, urinated upon, and allowed to wash it away only with your tears. Contemplate knowing that the dogs in the street have greater nourishment than you, who hunger for anything to kill the agony in your belly."[2]

Ramtha's mother was repeatedly raped. Different men, all anonymous, fathered her children, including Ramtha's younger brother and sister. Ramtha grew up scouring the streets for sustenance. When his mother and sister died, he cremated their bodies to keep them from desert scavengers. The funeral fire coalesced his hatred of the Atlanteans and of God, the great Unknown God, the impotent God worshipped by his people. The lonely fourteen-year-old boy escaped the city and found his way to a nearby mountain to confront God. Although God was silent to Ramtha's anger, a woman appeared and gave him a sword. It was a large sword, as big as the youthful Ramtha. She also spoke words of comfort and encouragement: "O Ram, you who are broken in spirit, your prayers have been heard." Then she added the cryptic words, "Take this sword and *conquer your-self*." He did not understand, yet he felt somehow affirmed by merely possessing the sword.

Although Ramtha had spoken with God's messenger, his anger had not dissipated. As he returned to Onai, other people joined him. By the time he reached home, he was leading what amounted to an army. The Atlanteans put up little resistance; they had forgotten how to fight. He and his ragtag army slew them and burned the city. He then turned over the food store-houses to the surviving Lemurians.

So emerged Ramtha the warrior. For the next decade his followers became a barbarian army. But Ramtha possessed a death wish. He led his army in battle after battle, always hoping that his next opponent would become the agent of his death. Instead, he became the victor who conquered tyrants. Finally, after years of wars, he was led into a trap. He was unarmed when an assassin stabbed him. And to ensure a slow death, he pulled the sword from Ramtha's body and left a gaping, bleeding hole. But Ramtha did not die. As he lay on the ground with his life draining out of him, a voice commanded, "Stand up! Stand up!" Slowly he responded. His enemies could not understand how he could rise. They decided he was immortal, turned, and fled. The event became the next turning point in Ramtha's life.

Ramtha now faced a lengthy healing process. He endured the feelings of helplessness, the loss of privacy, the stench of illness. He saw death and faced the impermanence of life. He watched the sun rise and set daily regardless of human events. Given time to contemplate life, Ramtha's thoughts returned to the God of his people.

RAMTHA'S TRANSFORMATION

Ramtha observed the world around him. He thought of the mythological gods and concluded that they were merely the symbols of human fears and desires. In contrast, the Unknown God was the ongoing essence that permitted humans, moment by moment, to create and live their illusions. Thus, the Unknown God was to be found in the ongoingness of the Life Force. God existed all around him. Ramtha's death wish left him, replaced by a desire to embrace life to the fullest. And a new, grandiose idea arose. What would it be like to be the Unknown God? Ramtha's spirit was lifted by that audacious thought, only to be brought back to reality by the wind, which blew his cloak over his head and then whipped up a cloud of dust that covered him.

Now Ramtha had a new focus for his consideration. He contemplated the wind, a powerful, unseen force that could come upon anyone. Even the most powerful could not fight it. It was ongoing, free-moving, without boundaries, limits, or form. It called Ramtha to be greater than any human had been, to exist unbound by human limitations such as death. The wind became his ideal.

19

After six years of focusing on the wind, Ramtha had what today would be called an out-of-body experience. His consciousness separated from his body, and he was in the heavens flying with the beloved wind while his body remained far below. Like the biblical Lot's wife, however, he looked back. Suddenly, fear overwhelmed him and he was thrown back into his body. It would take him seven years to repeat the experience. Only with effort did he learn to leave his body and become the wind at will. But he had taken a major step in accomplishing the task given to him by the woman of the sword. He was conquering himself.

As his desire to become the wind permeated his every thought, his bodily vibration (to use his term) changed. The slow, sluggish vibration of his physical body rose. He became lighter and took on a glow. Then one evening he rose with his body; it had become *light*. He exulted in the experience. Soon he soared upward again. And again. Finally, after more than sixty adventures moving in the sky realm, he concluded that his work on Earth was complete. He ended his earthly life by moving among his people and exhorting them to reach for what he had learned. He admonished them to place their faith not in him but in the God who made them all. Then he changed form for the last time. As his audience watched aghast, he became free of weight and time and form—and disappeared into a pulsating, invisible light. In his transformed state, he fully realized how limited he had been as a mere person. He had become a God.[3] Now, 35,000 years later, he came forth to teach all he has learned.

THE RAMTHA MYTH

It's a good story. At least, such was my initial reaction. But did it really happen? It could have, especially if one accepts the reality of Atlantis and Lemuria. Does it matter? Possibly. To Ramtha's critics, it matters very little. They do not accept his teachings, so there is little reason to consider this story as history. They merely pick a few elements to hold up for ridicule. To those who accept

Ramtha, the story is important, but not nearly as important as the teachings they have received and the relationships they have built with him. As with Bible-believing Christians and their belief in the stories of the book of Genesis, the faithful must struggle with the seeming contradictions between the "facts" asserted in the Ramtha story and the claims of modern science. There is little room for lost continents in the findings of modern geography or oceanography. However, just as the average Christian does not spend a great deal of time worrying about the historical actuality of Adam and Eve, so the average follower of Ramtha has little time to investigate the scientific credentials of Lemuria. Attention falls far more on the teachings and their ability to produce the promised life changes.

For the members of the movement, the Ramtha story has attained the same status as that of the movement of the Hebrew people in the Book of Mormon: it functions quite well as a religious myth. In this context, *myth* has a technical meaning quite apart from the popular use of the term, that is, an untrue story. Myth refers to a story that embodies a perspective on our ultimate concerns quite beyond the literal elements of the narrative, somewhat like the parables of Jesus. We often try to speak of ultimate truths in abstract terms, such as talking of God as omnipotent, omnipresent, and almighty. However, as an alternative, stories saying somewhat the same thing can often provide a richer way to speak of divine realities. In the end, as far as history and science are concerned, myth may be true, partially true, or complete fiction, but as myth it may be Truth. It tells a story about human life that resonates with the life experienced by the many people who accept it. It speaks of real emotions and feelings; it projects hopes and aspirations. It highlights a way of relating to the universe that gives meaning to life, whatever the other levels of truth or falsity may be.

Ramtha has built his teachings upon his own story, the implied assumption being "If I can do it so can you." And frequently he has expanded the myth with numerous stories about his life, which become immediate parables subtly illustrating his admonitions to his students. These stories also have become integral to the process of making the unseen Ramtha a real person to his students. Among his more moving stories is one entitled "A Gift of Freedom."

A young girl was brought into Ramtha's presence. In the land of his recently conquered enemy, she had been sexually abused since the age of four. As soon as she was old enough, she had become pregnant and had borne a son. She appeared ill-clad and was crying profusely, which made Ramtha very uncomfortable. During the course of his interrogation, her child, whom she had hidden in her clothes, dropped to the floor. Ramtha picked up the child. He was immediately taken by the child's beauty. He carefully unwrapped the child's clothes and held the naked infant aloft. The child laughed and then responded with a very childlike act: he urinated on Ramtha. Ramtha recovered his composure and continued to interrogate the very young mother.

"We are free here. You do not have to belong to anyone."

"But Lord, what should I do? I'm not gifted in craft, or scribe, or in the art of cookery."

"But you are gifted in the art of babes." (As he spoke, the child was enjoying himself exploring Ramtha's earlobe.)

"Lord, I beg you to rear my beloved son in your arms."

"Woman, but this is your freedom. Now you may have your son and do with him as you will. There is none that will make your life a misery." (Ramtha was now beginning to understand that she did not quite fit into his world.)

"No. No. My life is finished. I am an old woman, Lord."

Perplexed, Ramtha asked, "What does your freedom mean to you?"

"It is mine no longer, but that of my son's freedom. That is my freedom."

"What do you want me to do with your son?"

"To take him and rear him in your household." (As Ramtha continued to ponder the situation, the child continued to explore his face, oblivious of the words' implications.)

Finally, Ramtha arrived at a solution. "I will only accept this your son under one condition: that you be the entity that is the overseer of this son in my household, and I will call him *my* son and he will be motherless. You will be his guardian." The woman was elated, and he returned the child to the woman.

What lessons do his students learn from this story?

Freedom means . . . to be able to exult yourself whether it is in the self of another entity, into the greatest awareness that can be had. And that is what this little girl did with her little boy. . . .

The story of freedom you would say to me, "Ah but the greatest freedom is to have your baby without . . . the barbarian abusing you and the fear that the child would be abused." But her freedom was letting the child become a part . . . of something that had freed her to exercise the option to do with her prize as she wanted to. And her desire was to give it to me.

The story also illustrates a frequently encountered theme in Ramtha's stories in which Ramtha the conqueror took people otherwise subject to his power and became their teacher, helping them attain their wishes in life. However, that situation was somewhat reversed, as in the following story.

Following the destruction of Onai, Ramtha was confronted by Armenus, an older resident of the city. Ramtha invited him to join his army. The old man replied, "Young man, I must throw in with you, for I would find that it would be most direst in this state of affairs to go against one so outrageously powerful as you are. And I am not nearly the fool to see the end of my days, yet."

Ramtha asked him if he approved of the destruction of the city. He replied again diplomatically, "I am not quite sure I can either approve or disapprove, but one thing I cannot argue is that it has happened, and so with the results of what has happened, then I must conclude that it is meant to be, and wishing a man who likes to keep his head, I would want to be part of what is yet to become."

Ramtha immediately liked Armenus, and took him to be his own teacher and advisor. The old man taught Ramtha of the world and all its wisdom. He became a valued confidant for his ability to state his wise views without becoming emotionally involved.[4]

RAMTHA'S PRESENCE CONTINUES

The morning after Ramtha's initial appearance in JZ's kitchen, her son Chris reported a vivid dream in which hippies broke into the house and killed his stepfather and brother. JZ reacted immediately. Within a few days the family moved into another home. The next day they returned to their old home and found that it had been broken into and ransacked. Chris's dream had come true, and because of the prophecy, Ramtha's credibility level rose immensely.

Ramtha now began sharing with JZ basic information about himself and began teaching her concepts he would later teach publicly. But he also had to learn. He had lived so long in his unlimited existence that he had to remaster language, the limited means of communication he had left behind. He learned English so JZ (and later, others) could understand him.

Ramtha emerged as one of the most distinctive of non-embodied entities to speak, another factor setting him apart as a distinctive personality, so different from his host. His speech was peppered with the word *indeed* (heard repeatedly still when speaking with his students), a means of adding emphasis, much as *Amen* is used in some churches. As if unsure of the correct word to use, he frequently added phrases such as "that which is termed" and "as it were." As Ramtha became a public personality, his speech quickly became his most recognizable characteristic. His manner of speaking is amply illustrated by this paragraph from an early story:

And I sent her into that which is called the legion of women and there as it were indeed she was taken care of and quickly put to work. And there was an old woman as it were indeed who taught her to weave, who taught her to be as it were indeed skilled in the loom, and skilled in that which is called Mist Linen, a weaving process that is done under water. The woman began to glow, to come alive. And I have watched her, come and go. And always as it were indeed when she would get out into the sun, and she would pull back as it were indeed her hood and let her wondrous hair go free into the wind. She was beautiful.[5]

JZ began searching for someone to explain what was happening to her. She initially thought that perhaps Ramtha was a devil and sought help from several clergy, a most disappointing exercise. Unfortunately, most clergy are simply not taught, even in advanced pastoral counseling training, to deal with people who have had intense psychic experiences. Training in pastoral counseling assists clergy to recognize many forms of pathology, and often pathology provides the only categories into which they can place someone struggling with paranormal occurrences. Although these occurrences are unusual, even extraordinary, they are by no means symptomatic of illness, though the person who has them may or may not be otherwise healthy.

Eventually JZ found her way to the Rev. Lorraine Graham, a medium at a local Spiritualist church. During the course of their meeting, JZ went into trance and Ramtha began to speak through her. When he appeared, both Graham and Jeremy (who had accompanied JZ) noticed the change in JZ's body. Her posture altered and her whole body, especially her neck, seemed to expand. A peculiar smile appeared on her face. Ramtha reiterated what he had told JZ in their first meeting: that she would become a "great light unto this world." JZ then came out of the brief trance, not realizing what had happened. Jeremy and Graham explained that Ramtha had spoken through her, and JZ began a period of confronting Ramtha "possessing" her body.

Graham gave Jeremy and JZ a quick lesson in mediumship and related phenomena. She said JZ was an extraordinary medium, an opinion she had gained from observing other mediums in the Spiritualist movement. She also saw Ramtha as an entity of power. "Ramtha is like nothing that I have ever witnessed. Most spirits do not manifest themselves in broad daylight, and they don't open their eyes. And the touch . . . my dear child, it is known that you cannot touch a medium in a trance; it distorts the ectoplasm of the spirit and could easily kill the medium. But Ramtha touched me." In a later interview, Graham suggested that JZ should not be called a medium but was more properly referred to as a channel. "As I understand it," she said, "a channel leaves her body, as in death, and allows the entity to express his own personality. A medium serves only as a bridge between dimensions but does not entirely leave her body. It is a rare phenomenon for one to allow herself to be used like that."[6]

Because Graham accepted Ramtha, she provided much-needed social support for JZ during those early months. However, from a historical perspective of mediumship, Graham's understanding of the subject seems quite limited. Spiritualism created a peculiar teaching about the operation of mediums in darkness and the possible harm from touching a medium during a seance. Much of Spiritualism's opinions about mediumship was originated and perpetuated to protect the practice of fraudulent mediumship and to keep observers from interrupting fake séances and revealing the trickery. The attempt to fake psychical occurrences, although never the dominant practice within Spiritualism, became institutionalized in the movement during its earliest years; movement leaders, even those who would never participate in a faked event themselves, have done little to suppress it.[7]

Quite apart from operating in subdued light and refusing to be touched, mediums often follow eccentric practices. Some take off their shoes; others demand that flowers or a bowl of fresh

26
~

water be placed near them while they work. Such practices are not essential for the operation of a medium or channel. They derive from the process of learning to be mediums and mediums' attachments to ideas that their teachers told them were necessary or that seemed to provide support as they gained some control over and comfort with the operation of their mediumship.

Psychical researchers objectively observing mediums and channels fail to disclose any essential differences between them.[8] However, there is a range of mediumistic activity, that is, activity that attempts to allow contact between this world and disembodied entities. All entities—spirits of the departed, deities, Ascended Masters, master teachers, and space dwellers—speak and act through both mediums and channels. And both mediums and channels operate along the same spectrum of states of dissociation, from being fully awake and conscious all the way to full possession in which there is a complete loss of memory during the time that contact was established. The particularities of mediums and channels are often heavily influenced by their first teachers, who, consciously or not, pass along their eccentricities as if they were integral aspects of metaphysical truth.

When Ramtha appears, he completely takes over the operation of JZ's body. She is not conscious of what he does or says. Her change in body posture and facial expressions is noticeable to all who have observed her when she is in waking consciousness and when Ramtha is in control. The consistent personality differences between the two are always cited by people who know them as a major factor in their belief that Ramtha is a separate person. Mary Redhead, who was with Knight/Ramtha from the beginning and had seen several psychics develop during their early years, noted that JZ went through a long-term process of becoming comfortable with Ramtha's presence. She has suggested that perhaps when a few people unfamiliar with the process observed her struggle from a distance they confused it with rehearsing an act. JZ was, according to Redhead, going through periods of doubt and even anger. She had a strong ego

and fought to keep her personality from being dissipated or submerged. She also at times (even to the present) resented the
amount of consciousness lost and in her reveries occasionally
wondered if the purpose was worth the cost. In the privacy of her
own relationship, like Jacob and the angel she struggled with
Ramtha, the goal being the retention of her sense of selfhood
and, at times, her sanity.

Ramtha manifested as a full-blown secondary personality who
commanded much more of JZ's life than the average medium's
control. He is reminiscent of a few outstanding individuals in the
history of the paranormal. For example, William Sharp
(1856–1905) was a Scottish poet notable for his participation in
the Scottish Celtic literary revival of the late nineteenth century.
Many who read his books, however, were unaware of his second
life. Toward the end of the 1880s he began to manifest a secondary
personality, a female named Fiona Macleod. Like Sharp, she was a
writer, but her writing looked feminine and had a distinct literary
style. She also had a different personality and presence, which
Sharp's wife and the few friends who knew of her had no trouble
distinguishing from Sharp. His poet-friend William Butler Yeats
thought Sharp the most extraordinary psychic and was convinced
that "Fiona Macleod was a secondary personality—as distinct a
secondary personality as those one reads about in books of psychical research. At times he [Sharp] was really to all intents and
purposes a different being." He further described how Sharp would
"come and sit down by my fireside and talk, and I believe that
when 'Fiona Macleod' left the house he would have no recollec-
tion of what he had been saying to me." Sharp believed her a
distant cousin. Over several decades, Macleod wrote nine books,
which were critically acclaimed and became significant pieces of
the Celtic revival. Few readers or critics were aware of their
unusual origin, and Macleod even had a separate entry in the
annual British literary *Who's Who*.[9]

Macleod carried the memory of Sharp when she appeared,
but Sharp had no memory of her, only of lost time. She carried

on correspondences with people who were fans of her books and developed relationships with correspondents who were no part of Sharp's life.

Psychical research also documented several incidents of individuals who were the vehicles for a second "person" to emerge. For example, Patience Worth began to speak through Pearl Lenore Curran, a St. Louis housewife who was playing with a Ouija board. Worth wrote several novels, poems, and literary odds and ends. She spoke first in an archaic English, which became more "contemporary" as time passed. Those who sat with Worth over the years were convinced of her separate existence as a seventeenth-century person with a strong desire to be an author. Although Curran did not supply the proof for which psychical researchers were searching, she certainly convinced those who knew her that she was not Worth.

To those who have come to know him, Ramtha has the same kind of convincing presence, but there is little or no way to "prove" his existence in the manner appropriate to psychical research. However, noted researcher Walter Franklin Prince, in describing Curran, seemed to have summarized the question presented by entities like Fiona Macleod, Patience Worth, and Ramtha: "Either our concept of what we call the subconscious must be radically altered so as to include potencies of which we hitherto have had no knowledge or else some cause operating through but not originating in the subconscious of Mrs. Curran must be acknowledged."[10] Many parapsychologists have opted for the former, and as a result have concentrated their research on attempts to map the subconscious.

A RELIGIOUS MYTH BEGINS

But laying aside for a moment the question of Ramtha's objective reality, something important had begun: a new religious myth. It seemed at first glance to be what scholars call a world-denying myth, and several cursory observers have so taken it. In Ramtha's

29

story, ancient Atlantis became a metaphor for modern Western society: in love with technology, a society that places a low priority on the development of consciousness. It victimizes the Lemurians (some suffering in silence). Ramtha's family represents several responses: Ramtha's mother, like many people today, was a victim and suffered without being aware of an alternative. Ramtha, although not before the death of his mother and sister, found an alternative: he developed a hatred of the Atlantean way and withdrew from it for a time. However, he did not simply renounce society but used his time apart to mature.

Ramtha's story affirms a widespread belief that Western technological progress is not an altogether welcome reality. Modern life and the striving to possess everything to be happy can, like a tyrannical government, run roughshod over personal values and people's attempts to find their own happiness. In the 1950s, psychologists discovered that parents, teachers, the clergy, and even friends had united to push many middle-aged adults into lives that deep inside they did not want. Housewives yearned for office jobs. Professionals wanted to work with their hands. Teachers wanted to paint, and people writing ad copy wanted to write the great novel. And so, by the late 1970s they quickly responded to the story of someone who had found a new way of living and who provided the moral underpinning for making such a seemingly irresponsible decision as restructuring their lives.

But at the time that JZ began to allow this mysterious entity known only as Ramtha to speak through her, no one had any idea of the power inherent in the story he was about to tell and the work he was about to do. To understand, however, we must first turn to a discussion of Gnosticism.

3

MODERN
GNOSTICISM

At the time of its founding and in the years since, JZ has searched for the right term to describe Ramtha's school, frequently resorting to *esoteric* or *mystery*. But finally she labeled it "a modern Gnostic school." In so describing it she emphasized the fresh, unique philosophy and practice that Ramtha offered while claiming its rootedness in the primary alternative religious tradition that has shared space with Christianity in Western culture.

Gnosticism originated in the ancient Mediterranean Basin and has passed from community to community (many of its representatives being driven underground by persecution from Christian authorities). It found new life in the relative freedom of the post-Reformation era and has steadily moved toward reasserting the position it once enjoyed within the larger religious community. Understanding Ramtha by necessity includes some awareness of the tradition he represents. Those not ready for three centuries of Gnostic thought, however, can skip this chapter and return to it after the discussion of Ramtha's teachings and the practices at his school.[1] A survey of ancient and medieval Gnostic groups is in the appendix.

GNOSTICISM'S NEW BEGINNING

From its origin, the Gnostic movement spread throughout Europe and Asia, finding new expressions in popular teachers such as Valentinus, Basilades, and, most eminently, Mani. Mani's form of dualism spread from southern Europe to China and survives in parts of southern Asia to the present day. It was passed to medieval Europe by the Bogomils and Cathars and reached new heights among the Hermeticists, Jewish Kabbalists (and Christian Cabalists), and alchemists. Each movement flourished for a while, but all came under attack from the dominant social culture.

The Reformation restructured European society and in the process created a new situation ripe for a new wisdom. Columbus had discovered the New World, and armed with the pope's declaration of ownership, the Spanish and Portuguese had begun their invasions. Anticipation of further reform and discoveries was in the air. In the seventeenth century a modern Gnosticism—Rosicrucianism—offered one response to the changing world. In Rosicrucianism, a new element was added to the Gnostic tradition.

Previously, the Gnostic movements had found their authority in the writings of their founders. Rosicrucianism did not look to a contemporary founder but claimed access to a recovered ancient wisdom. Modern Gnostics would generally look to contemporary teachers who could expound a modern version of the ancient wisdom. Their accounts would follow one of three formats:

1. An individual would claim to have direct contact with the contemporary but hidden bearers of an ancient wisdom. That contact would take place in what to a modern Western audience was a remote and somewhat romantic area of the world. Arabia and Egypt remained popular into the twentieth century, but in the nineteenth century Tibet emerged as the most popular location. After absorbing the ancient teachings, the individual would return as a torchlight of wisdom. For example, sup-

posedly one Christian Rosencreutz traveled to Arabia and returned with the Rosicrucian teachings.

2. Someone would locate ancient texts (real or contrived) that contained the older wisdom now being revived. Thus, such texts would become the source of Hassidism, the modern Jewish ancient-wisdom movement.

3. Most frequently, the secret wisdom would be imparted from a noncorporeal realm, the home of the occult masters and inaccessible to the average person. In occultism, the Great White Brotherhood is the common designation for the Ascended Masters who still live on Earth and who have kept the faith through the centuries. At various times and places they appear to impart the ancient wisdom anew. Since the founding of the Theosophical Society in 1875 (discussed later in this chapter), the reports of contact with the Masters have been steadily increasing.

33

∼

THE ROSICRUCIANS

We shall probably never know the true reasons that compelled a little-known Lutheran pastor, Valentin Andrae (1586–1654), to write and circulate a series of works purporting to be the product of Christian Rosencreutz (C.R.).[2] In any case, in 1614 Andrae released a modest work, *The Fama Fraternitatis, or A Discovery of the Fraternity of the Most Laudable Order of the Rosy Cross*. It told the story of one C.R. who at the age of sixteen began to wander the world. Traveling to the Holy Land, Turkey, and finally Arabia, he learned of the ancient sacred and secret wisdom of the Near East. His pilgrimage then took him to Morocco, and at Fez he acquired mastery of the wisdom previously imparted to him.[3] He tried to give this wisdom to the learned of the world, only to be ridiculed. According to the *Fama*, only one, Paracelsus, the Swiss-born alchemist and physician, read the Latin translation of all C.R. had learned. Thus, Paracelsus attained his wisdom from C.R.

C.R. then settled in Germany and lived a quiet life. He had the prized philosopher's stone sought by the alchemists and thus could produce gold and jewels at will. He accepted only three students, later adding four more, to whom he taught all he knew. The students then agreed to the following:

- They would profess nothing but curing the sick without reward.
- They would wear no special habit.
- They would meet every year in the House Sancti Spiritus.
- They would choose their successors.
- The letters R.C. would be their only seal and character.
- They would remain secret for a hundred years.

Five students (now calling themselves brothers of an order) carried out philanthropic work. They traveled throughout Europe doing good works.

C.R. died in 1484 at the age of 106, the same year the pope issued his encyclical that launched the war on witches and sorcerers. He was buried in secrecy, the place of his entombment kept secret even from the other brothers. Some years later one brother "accidentally" discovered C.R.'s tomb, which bore the Latin inscription "After 120 years I will return." The brothers interpreted the inscription to mean that in 1604 the order should become a public organization and begin accepting all worthy applicants. Thus, 120 years later the order was revived and received its initial new members. Then in 1614 the *Fama* was published. It promised a sequel the next year.

That sequel, the *Confession*, also appeared anonymously. It offered commentary on Catholics and Muslims battling each other for control of Europe, the battle line at the time between Budapest and Vienna. It also attacked the decadent philosophy it saw dominating the world but promised a revival of enlightenment with the forthcoming wisdom.

The pamphlet pictured the order as a going concern. It would soon share with even the most humble the secrets it had discovered, secrets actually in nature and available to the observant. Among them were the alchemical processes of transmutation and the production of the universal medicine. Both could be created by natural means, but according to tradition the knowledge must not be abused by the merely curious and greedy.

The third volume of the original Rosicrucian trilogy, *The Hermetic Romance, or the Chemical Wedding, written in High Dutch by Christian Rosencreutz*, appeared in 1616. It was an allegorical autobiography of C.R. In it, for those aware of the coding, Andrae gave away his authorship by having C.R. don the traditional armorial bearings of the Andrae family. After the rather dry texts of the *Fama* and the *Confession*, *The Chemical Wedding* offered a delightful imaginal world permeated with alchemical symbolism.

In the beginning, C.R. finds himself in a dungeon. He and several fellow prisoners gain their freedom by climbing a rope lowered into the dungeon. He then puts on the Andrae-Rosicrucian emblems and begins the journey to the palace where the wedding of Silver and Gold is to occur. He carries salt, water, and bread with him. He travels through a fantasy land of beautiful maidens, symbolic castles, and mysterious inscriptions on golden tablets. He finally reaches the palace and the banquet hall, where others have previously gathered for the wedding. The next day all at the palace are judged against the weight of seven stones. Most are found unworthy and are dismissed. C.R. and the others found worthy are then allowed to attend the wedding.

The start of the strange affair is signaled by the appearance of the alchemical animals: a sword-wielding lion and a white unicorn. They walk down 365 steps and are adorned with garments representative of the Golden Sun and the Silvery Moon. Finally, they are presented to the king and witness a symbolic drama describing the seven stages of the hidden wisdom. In the drama, the king tries to rescue the queen from various afflictions, until at the seventh stage the wedding is finally begun. At this point, drama and reality come together. As a sense of dread overcomes the audience, the king and queen are beheaded. The guests must

35

now work for the pair's resurrection, accomplished with the blood of a phoenix. The king and queen are wrapped in velvet and carried to the wedding chamber where their union is consummated. They then join the others in a game in which virtues and vices are pitted against each other.

Unfortunately, shortly after the game the novel ends abruptly, as if the last pages had been torn out or the novel had been unfinished. The ultimate fate of the king, the queen, and especially C.R. were left to the reader's imagination. One can imagine the consternation. Many people read and reread the texts, looking for every nuance, every clue hinting at a method of contact.

The texts intrigued many who were eager to apply for membership in the brotherhood, which was just as eager to process new applicants. However, though people searched throughout Germany, and indeed the rest of Europe, no order was ever located. Among those who most anticipated the advent of the order was British alchemist Robert Fludd (1574–1637), who, unable to wait for formal contact, published A *Compendius Apology for the Fraternity of the Rosy Cross* in 1616, the same year *The Chemical Wedding* was published. He was soon joined by fellow countryman Michael Maiera, a self-appointed spokesperson of the order.

When attempts failed to discover the Rosicrucians who had written the three books, and the writings of Fludd and his contemporaries did little to call forth a response by the hidden brothers, several wrote books for the Rosicrucians and a few even began to found orders claiming Rosicrucian insights. From the original three texts, it was obvious that the Rosicrucians were close to the alchemists in thought, though they certainly denounced the charlatans then working in the courts of Europe. Some of the new "orders" emphasized the alchemical element, and others emphasized the possibilities of social reform and the coming of a new age. Among the many writers was the Abbé de Montfaucon de Villars (1635–1673), who in 1670 published one of the more famous titles in occult history, *Comte de Gabalis*. It circulated as an attack upon Rosicrucians but had the effect of causing a growth of interest in things occult by its Parisian readers. The abbé left the priesthood shortly after its publication and a few years later was murdered, by Rosicrucians, the rumors said, in vengeance for his having revealed the society's secrets.

In Germany, Rosicrucian ideals mixed with pietism. As the seventeenth century came to an end, Pietists, in their attempts to bring personal spirituality into the dry, ritualistic worship of Lutheran parishes, looked for the end of the world. Pietistic Rosicrucianism gave birth to the original American Rosicrucian group, a small group of occultists who settled in Germantown, Pennsylvania, in 1694. Known as the Woman in the Wilderness, the group under its leader Joannes Kelpius founded the first astrological observatory in the colonies so it could search the heavens for signs of Jesus' soon return and be the astrological consultant to Lutherans who wished to know auspicious moments for initiating important activities. When Jesus failed to appear and Kelpius sickened and died, the group gradually disbanded but passed on its wisdom to its neighbors. The beliefs still survive as the folk magic of southeastern Pennsylvania German-Americans.[4]

FREEMASONRY

Frequently neglected in the story of modern Gnostic development is Freemasonry. It has become a popular, largely secularized fraternity, whose emergence as an occult organization in the seventeenth century is largely irrelevant and probably unknown to the majority of its members.

Freemasonry (or Masonry) traces its origins to the stone-working craftsmen of the Middle Ages. They used the ancient-wisdom myth of Hiram in the Old Testament (I Kings 7:13–45), a significantly more acceptable source in Christian culture than the claimed Arabian and Muslim sources of Rosicrucianism. Hiram was employed by King Solomon to work on the temple in Jerusalem. Afterward, he disappeared from both the Bible and history. Freemasons, however, developed his biography. While

37

working on the temple, they decided, Hiram became aware of the "Word of God" inscribed in the secret parts of the temple. He would not reveal what he had learned and his artisan colleagues killed him. His death then became integral to the ritual initiation of members who symbolically die and are reborn into Masonry.

In the 1600s, however, the movement underwent a significant change as non-Masons founded societies loosely based on the older Masonic guilds. The idea may have sprung from the practice of some guilds to accept honorary members who were not stone workers. Several organizations, which consisted totally of such accepted Masons, appeared in Scotland in the mid-1600s. Some of these Masons admired aspects of medieval continental architecture, which they wished to introduce into buildings they were having constructed. A few, such as Elias Ashmole (1617–1692), mixed their love of architecture with an interest in alchemy, Hermetics, and Rosicrucianism. While trying to revive the architectural forms, they inserted the occult into the content of their lodges. Those lodges, in turn, became the basis of speculative Masonry, that form of Masonry which became completely divorced from any hint of attachment to a trade and focused upon the free-wheeling discussion of occult metaphysics. The only remnants of the mason's occupation were the use of the building arts as a metaphor for spiritual development, the symbolic use of the mason's tools (square, plumb line, compass, and level), and the wearing of aprons.

In 1717 four speculative lodges in London merged to create the Grand Lodge of England, whose influence quickly spread throughout Great Britain, into Ireland, and into Europe. Independent Scottish and Irish lodges formed a competing Ancient Grand Lodge, which united with the British Grand Lodge in 1818 to form the present United Grand Lodge.

Speculative Masonry claimed to present humanity's ancient religion. At one time, the Masons suggested, there were two religions, one for the educated and enlightened and one for the masses. The religion for the enlightened became the base upon which the religion for the masses (the various historic faiths) were built. Throughout the centuries, however, Adepts (Masters) kept the original secret teachings intact, and they were eventually passed in their purity to the Masonic leadership. Because of humanity's evolution, more people were now capable of receiving and safely handling that wisdom, which originally came from the ancient East and Middle East.[5]

Like other Gnostic teachings, Freemasonry embraces the concept of the seven planes or levels of existence, from the purely spiritual to the physical. It also believes that humans possess these levels and that all humans pass through all levels on their descent from the infinite unknown to Earth.

As important as Freemasonry's teachings have been to the Gnostic tradition, its organization has been equally significant. Masonic groups were organized into lodges, and their meeting halls were decorated in ways members imagined the old temple might have been. Temples frequently had murals of the Great Pyramid of Egypt, the monument of ancient building skills shown with seventy-two stones representing the seventy-two possible combinations of the four Hebrew letters of the name of God (YHWH), an echo of Kabbalistic traditions.[6]

They also instituted an initiatory degree system by which members were brought into the inner working of the lodge step-by-step. In the beginning there were three degrees, but so few degrees could never satisfy the true Gnostic. Elaborate systems of degrees were developed to picture the levels leading from this world to God and to symbolize the homeward journey of the knowing soul. Because of its success and longevity, the most famous was the thirty-three-degree system of the Ancient and Accepted Rite, which became integral to the dominant American Masonic body, the Ancient and Accepted Scottish Rite, as expounded by Albert Pike, its nineteenth-century intellectual leader.

Throughout the eighteenth century, Freemasonry aligned itself with the Enlightenment and with the antimonarchial ideals of late-century revolutionaries. Masonic and Rosicrucian ideals flowed through the salons of France and supplied vital ideological

39

components of the French Revolution. In Europe, Freemasonry has been intensely political. Its activities in France and Italy (Garibaldi was a Mason)—indeed everywhere—have earned the enmity of the Roman Catholic Church. Masonry's attackers have relished attempts to expose its position against Catholicism as the result of devil worship, Masonry's "true" occult secret.[7]

In America, James Madison, James Monroe, and Benjamin Franklin (who financed much of the American Revolution) as well as George Washington were Freemasons. The Masonic influence on the founding fathers is represented on the U.S. one-dollar bill, which hails the coming of the *novus ordo seclorum*, the "new order of the ages," and the pyramid topped with the all-seeing eye.

In post-revolutionary America, Freemasonry became staunchly nonpolitical, a factor that has allowed it to grow and become secular. Throughout U.S. history, Masonry attracted many who became political and cultural leaders. In the nineteenth century, as churches were shifting from rural to urban membership, many battles were fought over Masonry. Slowly, rules against secret societies were loosened and then discarded. Roman Catholics, burdened with an anti-Masonic stance by their Italian leadership, founded the Knights of Columbus, which could supply at least some of the benefits Masonry provided Protestants.

Most men joined the Masons for the fellowship and business opportunities it provided. However, Masonry teaches a very clear system of Gnosticism, and many Masons absorbed it, possibly without realizing what they were doing. Slowly, if they were also church members, they began to adopt a Gnostic interpretation of Christianity, and they found a way to get along in both worlds—the lodge and the congregation.

GNOSTICISM IN THE NINETEENTH CENTURY

Throughout the eighteenth and the first half of the nineteenth centuries, Freemasonry carried most of the Gnostic tradition, especially in English-speaking countries. Rosicrucian lodges appeared in prerevolutionary France, but the movement did not survive the revolution in a healthy condition. And Rosicrucianism was never a real force in England or its colonies. Sometimes Rosicrucianism was brought into Freemasonry, which, on occasion, then included a Rosicrucian degree in its speculative higher levels. The vacuum left by the lack of Rosicrucian organizations in the middle of the nineteenth century gave rise to a new generation of occult thinkers.

The first to assume responsibility for a revival of Rosicrucianism was an African-American Spiritualist, Paschal Beverly Randolph (1825–1875). Developing his thought initially as a variation on Spiritualism, Randolph claimed to have contacted and to have been initiated by the surviving Rosicrucian movement in France. He founded his first American Rosicrucian "lodge" in San Francisco in 1858, but the Rosicrucian fraternity had a shaky existence throughout Randolph's life, which included frequent moves, unstable income, and at least one fire that destroyed his library. The organization was not helped by Randolph's suicide. With his successors, however, it slowly began to stabilize, and it has become a strong organization proud of being the oldest in North America.[8]

A more substantive revival was initiated by British occultists who were members of a secularizing British Masonry. This effort may be directly based upon a German Masonic group, the Frates of the Golden and Rosy Cross. Also, members of the Societas Rosicruciana in Anglia had to be Masons. This group would become the source of similar organizations in Scotland and the United States. The American Societas Rosicruciana in Civitatibus Foederatis, founded by Masons in 1878, would later become the source of the Societas Rosicruciana in America, the second American Rosicrucian group to accept non-Masons into membership.

In 1909 Rosicrucian groups were joined by another new Rosicrucian body created by H. Spencer Lewis, who claimed independent French credentials to initiate a new order in America. Lewis not only opened his order to non-Masons but

41

also developed an active advertising campaign (which has continued to the present day) to recruit as many new members as possible. By the mid–twentieth century it had become the largest of all the Rosicrucian groups, now larger than all the others combined. The Ancient and Mystical Order of the Rosae Crucis claimed Egypt as the source of its ancient wisdom. Although a literal rendering of that claim may be in doubt, it has built a fine Egyptian museum in San Jose, California, which serves residents of California and the West Coast and supports some competent Egyptologists and their research.[9]

The Rosicrucian groups from Randolph to Lewis grew out of the Western Gnostic tradition by way of alchemy and Hermetics. Other groups—the first being the Rosicrucian Fellowship—were all founded in the twentieth century. Although still claiming the Rosicrucian name, these groups grew out of a separate occult tradition, a new philosophy that emerged at the end of the nineteenth century to connect Eastern teachings and Western esotericism—Theosophy.

THEOSOPHY AND THE MASTERS

Spiritualism had responded to nineteenth-century religious skepticism by claiming to demonstrate scientifically one of the major truths of religion, the continuation of the individual after death. While Spiritualist mediums concentrated on contacting spirits, other leaders in the movement were more interested in developing an all-encompassing philosophy out of the material the spirits revealed. From her contacts with entities she described as Masters, Russian émigré Helena P. Blavatsky brought together the common insights of Eastern philosophy and Western Gnosticism into a new synthesis informed by the new science of the era. It would become the most influential esoteric system in the West during the twentieth century.

Theosophy comprises a recognizable Gnostic system that begins with the Absolute, the unknowable, unmanifested destiny.

When the manifest universe finally comes into existence, it embraces the seven levels or planes of existence. These are distinguished by the density of the matter present on each level.

Madame Blavatsky, often referred to simply as HPB, will remain an enigma to the occult world. She emerged to the public as a participant in fake Spiritualist seances. Her flourishing career as a founder-leader of the Theosophical Society was all but destroyed by the exposé of continued fake mediumship tricks perpetuated in an effort to convince people of the nature and existence of the Masters, whose servant she claimed to be. Her system, which continues to inspire people unaware of her controversial past, has assumed a validity quite independent of the claimed physical manifestations of the Masters. Blavatsky's system was presented in a somewhat chaotic fashion, and her major work, *The Secret Doctrine*, is difficult to read. However, her intellectual successors, such as Curuppumullage Jinarajadasa, Annie Besant, and Charles W. Leadbeater, systematically laid out the teachings and constructed a distinctive theosophical theology.[10]

43

Theosophy is important for several reasons. One, it has become the most pervasive form of Gnostic occultism in the Western world. More than one hundred occult organizations can be traced directly to Theosophy, and they perpetuate its teachings or slight variations. The names of the overwhelming majority do not refer to Theosophy, and many adherents seem quite unaware of the theosophical heritage in which their groups are rooted. However, through the many books published by the Theosophical Society, the Gnostic tradition has been passed to the modern world where, in the contemporary atmosphere of religious and intellectual freedom, Gnosticism has been reborn.

Two, the Theosophical Society has also been the major factor in preparing the West for the influx and acceptance of Eastern ideas and spiritual practices. Such acceptance inspired the spread of belief in reincarnation and the revival of interest in astrology. For example, in the 1970s it was discovered that 20 to 30 percent of Westerners believed in reincarnation. That belief has built gradually over several decades. Throughout the same decades, Theosophy also provided a nurturing home for astrology, and many of the early leading astrologers began in theosophical lodges.

Three, theosophical teachings led to the New Age movement. One line of theosophical development passed from the Theosophical Society to Alice Bailey (1880–1947). A member of the society in California, Bailey began to channel material from one Master with whom Madame Blavatsky had been in contact. This channeling proved unacceptable to the Society's leadership, and she left to found her own organization, the Arcane School. She advocated the idea of a coming change—a new age—at the end of the twentieth century.

The resulting New Age movement helped popularize several theosophical ideas such as the notion that each person is God, an affirmation that sounds blasphemous to a theist who worships the One Almighty Deity but that has a much different connotation and its own rationale when affirmed by a Gnostic. The movement also provided a community in which channeling was encouraged and channels nurtured. Because theosophical Gnosticism provided the intellectual base for the New Age movement, it was not surprising to see the new channels teaching their variations as they assumed leadership positions in the movement.

Theosophy and the New Age have looked to science as an authority for their faith. Because a positive response to the implications of an expanding universe shown by the world of astronomy, the new psychologies, and quantum mechanics would undermine the basic worldview of traditional Theosophy, few have been willing to undertake the task of creating it anew. As we shall see, this task is exactly what Ramtha has assumed. His teachings can be seen as a next step in developing Gnosticism, notable in part for his consistent advocacy of some Gnostic implications for shaping the lifestyles of both the community of believers and the individual, which other Gnostic-oriented groups have avoided.

4

DEVELOPING
THE RAMTHA MYTH

Soon after JZ started channeling, she met Mary Redhead, a person knowledgeable of the psychic scene in the Pacific Northwest who took an immediate liking to JZ and was able to guide her through the psychic subculture. Since Redhead was not a psychic, she could become JZ's mentor without the distraction of being her competitor. Redhead began to take care of booking JZ's sessions, and within a few months JZ was experiencing the success that most psychics only dream about.

> Shortly after our debut at the Rama Center [in Seattle], my life started its unbelievable change from normal to chaotic. The phone started to ring off the hook with people asking for advice about their problems. People who just "happened to be in the neighborhood" started stopping by unannounced at any hour of the day. Often Mary [Redhead] brought people who wanted to discuss Ramtha and his phenomenon. In the midst of this, I tried feverishly to keep my house in order, serve everyone food, and tend to my family. Thank God for Mary, she ran herself ragged trying to help me.[1]

At one level the response was welcome; however, it also precipitated a major crisis.

A NEW ATTITUDE TOWARD MONEY

As JZ reflected upon the many people who now flocked around her, she concluded that the people who wanted time with Ramtha were vampires. They claimed they were seeking help, but they made no progress. They moved from one psychic reading to the next meditation session, only to pick up a taste of spiritual blood flowing from the psychic's veins. They took no responsibility, but they drained her of the time and energy allocated for her family.

JZ was ready to sever her relationship with both Ramtha and the world of spiritual seekers. The situation came to a head one afternoon while she was seeking a few minutes of peace and quiet. Ramtha suddenly appeared before her and in the ensuing conversation offered her an alternative solution. The next time the spiritual freeloaders show up, he suggested, "You are to ask for a tally of gold, when indeed, they come to learn."

JZ had arrived at the question all professional psychics, channels, and mediums eventually reach. Will I turn professional, and if I do, how will I handle financial remuneration for my services? There are several choices. They can remain amateurs and limit their psychic activities to their leisure time. They can become semiprofessional, accepting freewill gifts for their occasional work. They can turn professional. Some can work for an organization such as a Spiritualist church and draw a salary, but that is extremely difficult because there are almost no straight salaried positions not tied to performance. A few psychics find wealthy patrons, but such relationships rarely last for more than a few years. For all practical purposes, psychics are forced to be self-employed and must either charge a set fee or accept freewill offerings while "suggesting" amounts for their services.

In deciding to charge, JZ, like all religious professionals, confronted the larger issues relating to money, especially in a culture that pays lip service to the popular biblical (mis)quote, "Money is the root of all evil." The fact that money is a necessity, both to survival and to the accomplishment of many goals, as well as a temptation, has produced a certain schizophrenia in Western culture. On the one hand, we value giving to the church and have allowed some traditional religious organizations to become some of the wealthiest corporate entities in the West because of their tax-exempt status. And we have no problem with some religious leaders' salaries and wealth and with their ability to mobilize financial resources. On the other hand, we react negatively when religious leaders display their wealth or exercise the power in secular realms that their control of wealth supplies them.

Within the metaphysical and New Age community a different understanding of money prevails. Most practitioners teach what is termed prosperity consciousness. They believe that one's economic situation is in large part due to adherence (or lack of adherence) to certain metaphysical guidelines. Individuals have consciousnesses that dictate whether they will live in poverty or prosperity. People with poverty consciousnesses, for example, work at jobs and draw a minimal salary. People with prosperity consciousnesses tend to have careers and in different ways draw financial and other rewards to themselves according to their demands upon the universe. The perspective of prosperity consciousness has proven especially attractive to young business-people and the self-employed as a philosophical base that motivates them through the early lean years and allows them to fully enjoy increasing success.

Prosperity consciousness—the notion that teachers who practice what they teach will prosper financially and that poor people who present themselves as teachers are not living what they preach—has many ramifications for New Age metaphysical teachers and leaders. On the one hand, prosperity is a sign of success; on the other hand, any outward signs of success invite criticism both from the majority of people who do not share the perspective of prosperity consciousness and from less successful competitors.[2]

47

THE EARLY DIALOGUES

When JZ decided to turn professional and charge for her services, her life began to take on a more manageable structure. With Redhead operating informally as her manager, JZ was able to limit her public contacts to those who were more serious in their use of her skills.

JZ introduced Ramtha to the public in November 1978. He made his presence felt to the small group first by ruining their tape recording and then by giving each person a teaching, all the more impressive because he seemed to know each person's situation. Then on December 18, 1978, she held the first of what were termed Ramtha Dialogues in Redhead's Seattle home. Dialogues consisted of Ramtha making a presentation followed by a question and answer session. During the next year, word of Ramtha spread throughout the metaphysical world and JZ made trips east for dialogue sessions. It was at this time she began to wear the loose-fitting pants suits and Indian-style tunics in which she was most often photographed throughout the 1980s. With her hair pinned back in a ponytail, she became the image of the invisible Ramtha. She also received her first newspaper coverage; the feature article covering her New York dialogue appeared initially in *The Philadelphia Inquirer* but was afterward placed on the wire and reprinted in newspapers around the country. Author Fawn Vrazo described JZ as "a youngish woman of medium height with pale blond hair and dark roots. She is dressed in a deep blue velvet robe covered with gold braiding. She has an All-American cuteness about her, vaguely resembling Debbie Reynolds and Elizabeth Montgomery." She reported Ramtha's upbeat message that New Agers found so appealing:

> God is the creator of life. Indeed! An eloquent, pompous statement that speaks well of humanity. . . . You are not proclaimed bastards of an uncertain universe, but creations of the universe. Angels grander than

you? That is not how it is. There is nothing less than you and for certain nothing grander than you. . . . Long have you been separated from one another by races, creeds, religion. The father is one; indeed, you are one. Indeed! Never has the glory of God ever left you. The divine source presses to you everything you have ever wanted. All you have to do is feel it into being.

You want! Certainly. You need! Certainly. You desire! Certainly. How think you creation was created without this desire, to want, to need, to desire? What is the gift without understanding the giver? Indeed! You cannot deplete the supply called knowledge. Indeed! If you could, forever would never be. Everything you think is felt into reality. You are God. Simple. The source is God. You think it; He creates it. . . . You are forever, entity. . . . You will become one with the Source . . . the savior unto your own kingdom.[3]

49

Before the year was out, JZ was conducting Ramtha Dialogues around the country. Ramtha limited his appearances to between two and three hours; any longer left JZ exhausted as well as in an uncomfortable state she described as the twilight zone.

As the dialogues grew, the need to incorporate presented itself. Given the nature of the work, JZ founded the Church I AM, a nonprofit religious corporation, the most common form of organizing religion in America. However, it is a path fraught with difficulties for metaphysical and esoteric groups. The laws governing nonprofit religious corporations, including the most important tax regulations and the guidelines on what is a legitimate religion, are inherently Christian.[4] Also, many metaphysical groups do not consider themselves religions. They identify religion with rejected notions of church, established denominational structures, and academically trained religious leadership. New Age groups commonly draw a distinction between a religion (a church) and their spiritual organizations. Additionally, among metaphysical and esoteric groups, worship is at best a secondary activity. Their theology has little place for a theistic God (or Goddess), that is, a Supreme Being separate from and above creation who is both capable of receiving worship and desires such acknowledgment.

Finally, many spiritual groups wish to raise money by means other than by voluntary giving, which they view as tied to the constant begging for money. They also reject taking collections during group events such as occurs in many churches. New Agers frequently tie voluntary giving to a popular notion—that people do not value what they get for free.

The Ramtha organization considered these factors in making decisions throughout the early 1980s. The idea of a church was not compatible with their teachings, and after a few years they dissolved the Church I AM. JZ replaced it with a simple profit-making corporation. This structure seemed to align the older idea of prosperity consciousness with Ramtha's admonitions toward self-reliance and self-responsibility. The new corporate structure also established itself as a socially responsible organization. It paid taxes, thus contributing to the (national and local) community.

MORE PUBLICITY

Ramtha emerged to the public just as the New Age movement was being launched. Ramtha became one of the movement's stars.[5] JZ had no lack of attendees at the Ramtha Dialogues, for many people were looking for exactly what she was presenting. Then, in 1984 Jess Stern wrote a chapter on Ramtha in his book *Soul Mates*. In the book, Stern recounted the story of JZ's playing a grand piano. One night a short time after JZ had acquired a piano, beset with insomnia, she went to it and began to play. Jeremy and the children heard the music filtering through the house and saw her playing. Jeremy called in a neighbor who was a pianist. Listening to the previously untutored JZ, the neighbor exclaimed that it was the greatest piano he had ever heard. To JZ, the piano playing became a lesson of God's unlimited creative power. Stern also related the story of Ramtha's encounter with actress Joan Hackett. He spoke to her of an upswing in her career. "You will make more movies and you will win high honors in your profession. I will send you three offers in three days, and in one you will play a woman who is very like you. Have no fear. I will manifest it, so all will happen as I say."[6] She soon won the part in Neil Simon's *Only When I Laugh*, which landed her a nomination for both the Oscar and the Golden Globe awards.

Shirley MacLaine also spoke glowingly of Ramtha. MacLaine described her initial searches for spiritual understanding in her book *Out on a Limb*, and she also had conversations with Ramtha while writing it. Ramtha had encouraged her to write the book, against the advice of many of her associates, but he had opposed the negativism in the manuscript. He suggested that negative prophecies are often self-fulfilling. She would later see that this insight had been one of the most profound lessons for her since the beginning of her metaphysical searching. In a follow-up book, *Dancing in the Light*, she noted that her spiritual quest had taken her to many remarkable places where she met a number of "accredited mediums." "But," she added, "one was more profound than any of the others. His name was Ramtha." During their first meeting, Ramtha had picked her up in his arms and had carried her around the room. During the next months, she spoke with him separately. Ramtha told her that she had been his brother when he was living on Atlantis and related stories of their time together. "He humorously predicted personal events in my life—that always evolved to be true. . . . I asked questions relating to everything from the personal life of Jesus Christ to whether I would ever meet my soul mate in this incarnation. What I learned from Ramtha would fill another book. But no matter how much I learned from him, he continually reminded me that *I* already knew all of the answers." Ramtha also had advised her to turn down offers for two movies and wait for a third. "You will not only win the highest award for this coming picture, but you will bring great enlightenment to the

51

world with your writings." The movie was *Terms of Endearment*, one of MacLaine's most heralded performances.[7]

Word that JZ was the preferred channel for the stars in Hollywood brought more people to Ramtha. By 1984 the earlier dialogues had evolved into weekend intensives, and the first retreats were held in the desert at Yucca Valley, California, that same year. In 1986 the first of the advanced intensives, at which Ramtha spoke at length on topics of special interest, was held. A variety of programs was offered, including workshops and the more informal "days with Ramtha." Some intensives were video-taped and released in a video series still available in New Age bookstores. A series of books, most derived from transcribed texts of various events, was published.

The first reaction to Ramtha from the secular press had been dominated by a sense of curiosity at channeling, this new (to the average reporter), exotic form of religion. Channeling in general and JZ in particular had been met with some degree of skepticism and humor. For example, the grocery-store tabloid *Weekly World News* of May 24, 1983, informed its readers, "A 35,000-year-old Spirit from a lost civilization lives again within the body of an ordinary American housewife." But as channeling spread, as celebrities identified with it, and then as several channelers clearly emerged as leaders in popularity and financial success, the amount of attention paid increased proportionally. By 1987 observers were aware that channeling was more than just a pass-ing fad. They were not prepared for the response to the television presentation of Shirley MacLaine's autobiographical *Out on a Limb*. Channeling and the New Age movement were no longer just an interesting curiosity on the fringe; they moved to the cover of *Time* and threatened to become a new Spiritualism, a new reli-gious movement that had far greater potential to win the minds and hearts of the public than did religions coming from the East.

Robin Westen, in her book *Channelers: A New Age Directory*, spoke of JZ as "one of the most celebrated of current channels." She noted that in the early 1980s, "Ramtha's words began spreading like wildfire, spearheading the current channeling movement."[8] The initial public image of Knight/Ramtha was as New Age channeler and channeled entity. That image led to an appearance on the Merv Griffin Show in 1985 and to my inclusion of Knight/Ramtha in my 1990 *New Age Encyclopedia*, among many other references. It has been an image hard to shake.

WHAT IS CHANNELING?

Channeling, a process by which information is accessed and expressed by someone (the channel) from a source other than ordinary consciousness and memory, has an old and honored tradition in the West as well as in ancient Egypt, Greece, and the Near East. Although most contemporary Jews and Christians are loathe to think of the biblical prophets as channelers, the term fits them perfectly. The prophet (or channel) received words from the Transcendent One (who becomes the channeled entity) and spoke those words to the waiting audience. The New Testament provided what many New Agers consider an almost textbook example of channeling, the Book of Revelation. John, who wrote the book, claimed not to be the author. Rather, he asserted,

> I was in the Spirit on the Lord's Day and heard behind me a great voice, as of a trumpet, saying, I am Alpha and Omega, the first and the last: and, What thou seest, write in a book, and send it unto the seven churches which are in Asia. . . . (Rev. 1:10–11)

Being "in the Spirit" appears to be what today we would call entering an altered state of consciousness. John heard a voice speaking to him, and in the remainder of the Revelation reported what he saw while "in the Spirit."

Over the centuries channeling has had a checkered career. After possibly reaching its lowest point in the eighteenth century, it reappeared in strength in nineteenth-century Spiritualism. Much

of the writings of Spiritualist founder Andrew Jackson Davis consisted of channeled material. As Spiritualism matured, two outstanding channeled works appeared.[9] Channeling existed apart
from the primary thrust of Spiritualism, which centered upon facilitating contact—through mediums—between members and those
who had passed beyond the grave. Although many Spiritualist
mediums also operated as channels, it was a secondary activity for
most. From the 1880s into the mid–twentieth century, psychical
research actively studied Spiritualism and pressed the case for valid
"evidential" material to substantiate claims of spirit contact. Channeling, which tended to emphasize philosophical teachings by
exalted beings, did not produce material or activities that readily
yielded verifiable material; hence, except for a few prominent
exceptions, psychical researchers never seriously considered it.

Throughout the twentieth century, a variety of channels
(many who do not favor or use the term) produced information
from different entities. A few built quite substantial organizations, the most famous being Edgar Cayce. Alice A. Bailey
channeled the theosophical master Djwhal Khul, and Guy W.
Ballard launched the I AM Religious Activity by channeling
messages from Saint Germain and other Ascended Masters.[10]

A new wave of channeling began in the 1950s within the
flying saucer contactee movement. Although the earliest individuals claiming contact with flying saucers seemed to be claiming
face-to-face contact with saucer pilots, increasingly, contactees
were channelers who brought through metaphysical messages. It
would, in fact, be among the contactees that the modern term
channeling was first used. The contactees would serve as a bridge to
the New Age movement by identifying the older theosophical
masters with the leadership of the intergalactic space command.[11]

In the 1950s also, mediumship developed a negative image
for many people because of the seemingly passive role (loss of
control while in a trance) mediums assumed in the spirit communication process. Many mediums (or channels) responded by
developing forms of mediumship that required no trance state or

54
∾

loss of consciousness, which, throughout the 1960s and 1970s, set the stage for a new generation of seekers who were less concerned about the control issue and more interested in the dramatic and startling effects of trance phenomena.

Mediums operate along a spectrum of altered states of consciousness. At one end, some awareness of what is occurring is apparent; at the other end is total unconsciousness. Some channels are fully awake but hear a voice speaking to them that they, in turn, convey to listeners. Such channeling is like the inspiration that comes to artists or musicians, who put colorful visions on canvas or "hear" their compositions before writing them. Channels in this slightly altered state may, at times, relay questions to the entities they channel. Other channels enter a partially dissociative state and engage in automatic writing. Although their hands move by unconscious control, they may be otherwise fully aware.

At a deeper level, channels may enter what can best be described as a dissociative state (a light trance) and while awake and aware allow channeled entities to respond directly through them without their verbal intervention. Others go into a more complete trance and turn over control of their bodies to the channeled entities, though they remain conscious. Their consciousnesses may be inside their skulls, slightly outside (behind and above) their bodies observing what is occurring, or completely away from their bodies. Channels in a trance state have reported viewing a channeling session from different points in the room (as in classic astral projection or out-or-body experiences), or they may be taken far away from where the channeling occurs. Many channels relate that during channeling sessions their consciousnesses go elsewhere and they receive instruction from colleagues of the channeled entities. Many channels are simply unconscious during the channeling activity.

A new era in channeling began in the 1970s with the issuance of *The Seth Material*, a volume of lessons claimed to be channeled through Elmira, New York, housewife-writer Jane

55

Roberts (1929–1984). Roberts (the pen name of Jane Butts) and her husband had experimented as early as 1963 with a Ouija board. Seth, a disembodied entity, communicated through the board; soon afterward Roberts discovered her ability to go into trance and have Seth speak through her. Her husband recorded the sessions, which were later transcribed and used in her first nonfiction book, *How to Develop Your ESP.* However, it was not until *The Seth Material* in 1970 that Seth and Roberts caught on.

Seth emerged as a popular spiritual teacher in spite of Roberts's reluctance to become a public personality. She continued her channeling activity quietly, almost never accepted invitations to speak to her waiting public, and took no steps to organize the many students of the Seth material. She did create a public who yearned for personal contact with a channel, and by the end of the 1970s many, including JZ, had appeared.[12]

JZ AS CHANNELER

When JZ channels, she is completely unconscious during the time Ramtha inhabits her body. As Ramtha informed his students, "My daughter JZ, who graciously allows me to use her embodiment, is what is termed a pure 'channel' for that essence that I am. When I speak to you she is no longer within her body, for her soul and spirit have left it completely."[13] After the sessions she is unaware of anything Ramtha said and is dependent upon others for a report, especially if he said something she will be responsible for implementing. At the height of her traveling in the 1980s, she lost as many as 150 days a year while Ramtha spoke. Yet she also believes that she, at least some of that time, was receiving instructions while Ramtha was speaking but was consciously unaware of her lessons.

JZ is thus what some term a full-body channel, in that Ramtha takes control of her body completely. Many people report seeing changes in her body as she moves from her control to Ramtha's. Her body seems to swell and she reports that it retains water.[14] The obvious change in facial expression and vocal tonation is apparent to any who knows JZ when Ramtha is not present. During the several years I have known her and have observed Ramtha, I also have observed other differences. For example, JZ is very feminine, though she can be a most determined person while pursuing important goals. A wide range of emotions, expressed most clearly in her likes and dislikes, lies close to the surface ready to emerge at a moment's notice, and she can be quite blunt in heaping praise upon or expressing disappointment with her associates. These emotions come forth clearly whenever she speaks of her childhood or of the vicious attacks that have appeared in the press.

Ramtha, on the other hand, is a dominant, patriarchal figure. Whether dressed in the white flowing robes he generally wore in the 1970s or in the loose-fitting garments, baseball cap, and boots he prefers at present, he is a commanding figure. He enters the teaching center to the adulation of his students and teaches them as someone possessed of the truth. He will, in the course of a three-hour session, cajole, shame, and congratulate his students. Although he criticizes them, at times harshly, he is even more free with his praise. He has a ready sense of humor and frequently makes jokes to point out a common failing or to reclaim the attention of those lost in his philosophical abstractions.

RAMTHA'S TEACHINGS

Ramtha's books and videos also present a comprehensive picture of the primary ideas he shared with early students, including a discussion of his role. He said that they had forgotten their heritage and that they needed to stand up, throw off their bonds of limitation, and reclaim their lives as divine beings. He reminded them of the truth of their lives. Although he shared the story of his life and enlightenment as a means of establishing his authority, he frequently reiterated,

57

I am not here to be worshipped or to be idolized or to be sought after. I am to be loved. I wish none to sit at my feet but to look me in the eye. I wish to exalt all men as I have been exalted. I wish no followers, only leaders. And I will not free you, but you will by your own conviction that you are, and that be better indeed.

I am not a sage, I am not a fortuneteller, I am not a priest. I am but a teacher, servant, brother unto you.[15]

The truth of this position is difficult for many observers to comprehend. America has become home to many gurus and messiah figures seeking to impose sets of beliefs and, of more importance, systems of behavior on their followers. Thus, there is a tendency for observers—especially those who do not have the opportunity to study groups firsthand and see the differences—to approach new groups by looking for a catalogue of beliefs and a list of behavior rules. They can't deal with an open system in which the teachings do not tell adherents how to act but provide a context in which lifestyle choices can be made. Among Ramtha's students the ability to make choices is valued, but the nature of those choices is neither dictated nor judged.[16]

Many, however, saw Ramtha as a fountain of wisdom who could tell them how to live. They liked his basic theological alternative, and they read the books, watched the videos, and attended the intensives. They expected Ramtha to answer every question, and Ramtha on occasion helped people by discussing their situations. Many were astounded by the accurate predictions he occasionally made. However, Ramtha refrained from dictating choice. His primary approach is more clearly revealed in the following dialogue between Ramtha and a frustrated young man (the master):

Master: Well, I really don't have any questions to ask you. Actually, I have mixed emotions about being here. A friend told me about you and how meaningful it is to come to your audience. But frankly, I find this all pretty boring. I haven't heard anything I don't already know, only a bunch of glib answers to some petty problems. At times I think that everybody here has got to be absolutely insane for being here.

Ramtha: Then why do you stay?

Master: That is a good question. I think it is because I keep waiting to hear something that applies to me.

Ramtha: Master, never go against your feelings and stay with something that bores you, when you could be experiencing life and its adventures. If you are bored, and yet you stay, you are living in a state of great duality and disharmony, which one should never do. If you are bored, you should certainly go from this place, straightaway, and find a challenge that brings you joy. To stay with something that bores you is being a fool. If you wish to express as a fool, be happy to be known as that, and do not complain.[17]

59

Ramtha operates as a catalyst for individuals to discover and manifest their own masterhood. Humble worshippers who hang on his every word would defeat the purpose of his teachings. As people understand Ramtha's worldview, they show respect for him out of thankfulness for the insights he gives them. However, their advancing autonomy leaves no place for the kind of adulation common from followers of Eastern gurus.

RELIGION AND GOD

Ramtha also contrasted his teachings with those of Christianity. JZ had concluded that Christianity had seriously erred, especially on its ideas of sin, hell, and damnation, and Ramtha confirmed her belief. In one of his early sessions he stated,

The greatest thing that which is termed religious orders or the Church did to *un*enlighten this plane is that they took God outside of Man, put Him outside, far, far away. They separated Man from his divinity in order to enslave him. You have been a product of that.

Ramtha complained that the church enslaved individuals through their ignorance, its rules and regulations, and its erroneous view of the world. At times he hinted that the church was a knowing repressor of its members, as with its teaching on poverty:

> The Church has been a form of great tyranny, because it has suppressed people and kept them ignorant for many centuries. Through its dogma, it has taught them that to find God, you cannot be the rich man. This teaching has been a very clever design to give great power to the Church. If you keep a man suppressed by removing his treasury, giving him a little ground to work, and then forcing him to give the best of his yield to the Church, you will always have dominion over him, always. Then man, the god, the creature birthed in freedom to live in freedom, becomes the enslaved, the wretched.

His harshest words were reserved for the church's manipulation of fear as a social control tool:

> I will tell you a great truth: Man has created images of God that he could use to control his brothers. Religions were created to control people and nations when armies failed, and fear was the tool that kept them in line. If you take divinity out of any man—take God out of him—then you can easily rule and control him.

> God has not created hell or a devil. These were dreadful creatures of man to torment his brothers. They were cre-

ated through religious dogma for the purpose of intimidating the masses into a controllable organization. That
is a great truth.[18]

One can argue with Ramtha's understanding of the origins
and function of the doctrine of hell or the devil in Christian
thinking, or the reasons for the church's identification with the
poor. However, it is undeniable that many clergy have used the
fear of the devil or hell to hold church members and enforce various behaviors. It is equally true that negative reactions to such
manipulations have not only been a significant factor in the
founding of alternative religious groups throughout the twentieth
century but also that disagreement over the prominence given to
hell and the devil figured importantly in the split between fun-
damentalists and modernists within denominations.

Traditionally, Christianity posits a transcendent deity who
created the world, including human beings who are expected to
acknowledge the Almighty through worship and obedience.
God's power sustains the world at every minute. Sin, the human
problem, is viewed as separation from God and God's plan for
humanity. Humans are saved and brought back into a personal
relationship to God by their trust in the atoning work of Jesus the
Messiah. The Holy Spirit dwells within Christians manifested as
God immediately present.

61

Ramtha differs from traditional orthodox Christianity at
almost every point, beginning with his denial of God as a personal Creator existing apart from creation. Rather, he asserts,
"God is an all-consuming force that is everything. . . . God is not
a singular character who sits upon a throne and judges the whole
of life. God is the whole of life—*every pulsating moment*. It is the
ongoingness and foreverness of everything that is." In telling his
story, Ramtha spoke of the Unknown God, whom he likened
unto the wind. "It was not the wind I became," he noted, "but the
ideal that the wind represented to me. . . . I became the unseen
principle that is free and omnipresent and one with all of life. It

was when I became that principle that I understood the Unknown God and all that it is—and all that it isn't—because that is what I wanted to understand."[19]

Ramtha clarified his understanding of God in his myth of creation. In the beginning, in so far as a beginning can be posited, all that existed was the infinity of Thought, which Ramtha refers to as God, the Father. Thought is the principle cause and foundation of life. God was Thought without form, but Thought then contemplated itself. When Thought contemplated Thought, God *expanded* into a unique form of himself. According to Ramtha, anytime thought is contemplated, the action of pure reasoning expands the thought—the thought becomes *more*, it becomes greater. The act of contemplation occurred because of *Love*. Love is best understood as God's desire to find expression in the ongoingness of creation. Thought, via contemplation of itself, expanded into the principle of Thought termed *Light*. Whenever thought is contemplated, it first expands and then is always *lowered* into a vibratory frequency that emits light.

Humanity originated in the birthing of Light. Light came into existence as a multitude of *particums* of Light, and each particum (protoparticles that appear in the early stages of the creation process) became an individual, a son of God, a light being. Everyone was created at the same time, as a Light form, participating in the essence of Thought. Each person is the divine Light, the original and permanent body, the Mind of God in singular form. The soul was created for the purpose of capturing and holding Thought and Love as it flowed from God the Father and putting it into memory in the form of feelings. The individual's soul is housed within its spirit and enables the individual to be a creative principle. God the Father manifests Love in granting free will to each individual to explore the totality of Thought.

The particums of Light thus became the creators of the universe. First, they contemplated themselves, then contemplated the ideal of Light into matter, the result being the formation of billions of suns (stars). Creation always proceeds by a similar process. The individual soul contemplates an idea. The idea expands into very high frequency light, which is then lowered or slowed, first to become *electrum* (existence in an electromagnetic field with a positive-negative polarity), which, in turn, coagulates into gross matter. Gross matter, in turn, coagulates into molecular and cellular structures—basic forms. These forms follow the thoughts originally contemplated by the light beings.

The light beings created all of what we now know as the universe, from all the elements to all the life forms that have existed and now exist. It is thus proper to think of each light being as a god with a small g. It is proper to state that God, with a capital G, did not create the universe. Rather, God *is* the universe; we, the gods, created all things of the universe by thought and contemplation. The ongoingness of the universe is the process of the continued expansion of God by the gods.

At one point many of the gods—the light beings—came to Earth and created and evolved all its life forms. As Ramtha put it, "Over millions of years, as you know time to be, you took from the Thought that the Father is, and through your supreme intelligence and creative power you designed your ideals of creation." What we now know as the geologic record is a presentation of the evolution of thoughts, which began to create mere globs of simple forms and proceeded to bacteria, simple plants and animals, and, finally, more complex life forms. After a type of creature appeared, an array of varieties evolved from it. Colors and smells were introduced. New species were given patterns of genetic memory that allowed each to reproduce and evolve.

As life evolved and a food chain was created, light beings decided to create a vehicle through which they could both directly experience their creation and continue to express their creativity. They had encountered a problem with original creation; although they could, so to speak, become the flower, they could not relate to it as physical beings. They could not smell it or touch a tree or appreciate the beauty of the colorful landscapes they were manufacturing. The result was the first hominoid creature, a vehicle of

63

matter for the gods. Its body could hold the soul and be enveloped by the spirit. The soul could then record and store the experiences of the body as feelings, a permanent record of its lively experiment. As the gods took embodiment in gross matter form, they became what is properly termed god-men or men-gods, "God" expressing in human form. The body continuously evolved; over ten and one-half million years (a record being uncovered in fossil form) it was perfected. It is thus rather young, a product of only a few million years of evolution. But the light beings that are the true essence of humans are quite old, having existed since time began.

From this creation story, Ramtha students perceive the essential mythical truth that each individual is God manifested as human in order to continue the expansion of Thought (God, the Father) into eternity. Inherent in the human condition is not just the ability and the drive to create but continually to re-create the world.

64

THE POWER TO CREATE

No single idea so permeated the New Age movement as the notion that we create our own reality. This idea can have a variety of meanings and implications, but at its basic level it is experienced in social relationships—in the manner in which we construct our social worlds and the sometimes dramatic changes that can occur as we change our opinions about life, other people, and the nature of the universe. I first saw people actively reconstructing their social environments while observing life in a small holiness church in Illinois in the mid-1960s. Week after week members gave testimonies of their new lives since receiving what they conceived to be the Holy Spirit in their lives. I heard stories of changed relationships, especially their job relationships. People noticed the difference. They arrived on time, gave a full day's work, and left only after the workday was complete. Soon they were receiving raises and promotions. Their self-esteem improved, and they found themselves on an upward spiral in which their inner attitudes led to positive changes that, in turn, strengthened their inner attitudes, leading to further changes.

Within the metaphysical churches such as the Unity School of Christianity and the Church of Religious Science, a great deal of thought is given to the process of changing one's world. The Declaration of Principles of the International New Thought Alliance affirms a belief, for example, "that man's mental states are carried forward into manifestation and become his experience through the Creative Law of Cause and Effects." Thus, insofar as we can attune ourselves to God, such negativities as illness, poverty, and unhappiness will disappear.[20]

Ramtha, initially at least, based his understanding of our ability to re-create our worlds on his understanding of human beings as essentially light beings expressing themselves in and through gross matter. The purpose of embodiment is more completely to comprehend the inclusive nature of God. And Ramtha celebrates the individual. He or she

65

> *is* the image of God, the duplicate of what the Father is. The essence that you are *is* that which is ongoing, ever evolving, ever changing, ever creating, ever being. You are thought, you are light, you are electrum, you are form. You are pure energy, awesome power, pulsating emotion, sublime thought. That which you have perceived to be the highest level of intelligence, of power, dignity, holiness and grace, is that which is you. Who are *you?* You are "the identifiable God."[21]

SIN OR IGNORANCE?

However, soon after the light beings embodied themselves in matter, a problem developed. At first they understood their divine state and lived in a single body for many thousands of years. The purity of unlimited thought gave the body immortality. However, in the delight of experiencing the new playland of matter, individuals began to forget their divinity. Savoring life and creating new things to delight the mind and senses, the unlimited entity began to experience and contemplate limitations and to hold such limited ideals as jealousy, survival, and possessiveness. The body began to express the limited thoughts and concerns entertained by the mind of the embodied being. Ramtha described the process as a downward spiral.

> When God-man began to experience attitudes of survival, he began to lessen his power of thought to spark an eternal life-force within the body. Thus, the body began to fail. As the body began to fail, it lessened man's ability to reason through the brain. As man began to lose his power to reason, fear began to engross his consciousness. As the element of fear became an attitude within man's thought processes, the embodiment began to suffer from the force and effects of fear, disease, illness . . . death.[22]

66

The experience of limitation locked the beings in the bodily experience. After death, they possessed only one avenue of continued advancement in life: the return to the embodied experience. Beings returned through the seed of their own offspring. However, the process of falling deeper and deeper into limitation continued and gradually they forgot their divinity; this plane became the whole concept of life. In their limitation, they became fearful and herdlike, and as a result subject to people who claimed mystical knowledge and spiritual insight. Thus, religion, preaching the separateness of God and humanity, emerged, controlling and ruling people by its oppressive ideas. Given the soul's memory of the ideas of limitation, fed to it over many lifetimes, limitation became its reality, the steadfast pattern of thinking wedded to the soul memory. Such deeply embedded patterns are no easy matter to change. Incarnation, intended to be a game, became a trap. Having lost the knowledge of their divine unlimited nature, humans have been doomed to reincarnate in ignorance forever or at least until that memory of divinity can be restored.

Ramtha's basic teachings fit very comfortably into the larger New Age world, although there were some minor points of conflict. For example, he downplayed karma and astrology: in the long run they were simply additional systems of limitation as alienating as religion was. Humans were here solely to experience life in the material world and to exercise their creativity. This basic message was repeated over and over in slightly different ways, and it found a significant response within the New Age community. His advanced intensives explored the implications of students' lives, from sexuality to coming world changes. Some students, after attending the lectures and workshops, began their own careers as New Age channels and teachers. Most of his faithful followers returned to their more or less mundane existences with lives only slightly altered, not essentially changed. Many remained for what may be thought of as the wrong reasons—they liked Knight/Ramtha, or they affirmed the basic tenets of the philosophy, or they had found a compatible group of friends with whom to socialize. But they gave little thought to the crucial aspects of the teachings.

The real world, dominated by limitations of all kinds, still controlled perceptions. It was so ingrained that merely the acceptance of Ramtha's ideas did little to lead the students to masterhood. Masterhood remained a carrot that moved just beyond arm's reach on the few occasions any dared reach out to grasp it.

RECOUNTING THE RAMTHA MYTH

In 1987, almost a decade after meeting Ramtha, JZ wrote *A State of Mind: My Story* with several goals in mind. She wanted to tell her side of what had become a most controversial story. She was under attack from the media, and she, like most of us, wanted at least to be understood, if not liked. She believed absolutely in the reality of Ramtha and wanted to communicate to readers that she was neither naive nor crazy but had a carefully thought-out rationale based upon extraordinary events that had convinced her Ramtha was literally who he said he was. But she had little realization that, more important, in recounting her life she was providing a modern illustration of the Ramtha myth.[23]

She seemed to have it all. She was the wife of a well-to-do professional man. She had two children about whom she had the strongest of maternal instincts. But she had been ultimately unhappy and unfulfilled until Ramtha came to help her "over the ditch." Given all that occurred after he entered her life, at times she might have been tempted to say that Ramtha had "grabbed her and drug her through the ditch" rather than play the Sir Walter Raleigh role and gallantly provide a cloak to ease her passage. However, she could not deny that Ramtha did give her a point from which she could begin to restructure her existence.

Like Ramtha's mother, JZ had been a victim. Like Ramtha, she also possessed resources, "Lemurian" resources. She had some openness to an inner world passed on from her mother. Rather than being crushed by life as had many raised in poverty, even without the college education she had so wanted, she successfully realized the American dream. But the dream was not fulfilling, at least to her. She wanted something more. Ramtha appeared to lead her to something more, that additional something that is so valuable that one is willing to risk all one possesses to have it. It is a story almost biblical in the way it speaks to anyone, of whatever socioeconomic status, who feels trapped by an idol, a false god that offers everything but ultimately cannot deliver.

In years to come, those who read religious biography will, whether they respond to her message or not, place JZ's account beside stories of other powerful American women, including Anne Hutchinson of the Massachusetts colony and Shaker leader Ann Lee and, more recently, Mary Baker Eddy, Emma Curtis Hopkins, Alma White, Aimee Semple McPherson, and Kathryn Kuhlman. Each was denied a place in the religious community of her childhood; each had a life that itself embodied with all its ambiguities the message she later articulated; and each spoke powerfully to a group of her contemporaries in such a way that the larger community could little comprehend. Each illustrates the continuing appeal of myth to relate to and affirm the basic story from which we construct our personal worlds.

THE SCHOOL'S FORMATION

By the mid-1980s Ramtha's movement seemed to reach critical mass. The number of people attending the events steadily increased. In 1983 the first two volumes of what would be a series of books based on Ramtha's transcribed teachings were released; the following year the first of several videos of dialogue sessions, *Audience with Ramtha*, appeared. Many people unable to attend dialogue sessions learned of Ramtha and his teachings through these materials. Channeling had spread throughout the New Age movement, and many channelers could be found in every city. Of those, some found a national following, justifying commercial publishing of their channeled material. A few became nationally known through widespread media coverage and were invited to appear on national television shows. Of these, Ramtha emerged as the acknowledged leader of the pack. In June 1986 the *New Age Journal*, the leading periodical of the movement, described JZ as the heir to the late Jane Roberts.[24]

Throughout 1986 and 1987, Ramtha publications increased and sold well. In the wake of national media coverage, large groups (three hundred to seven hundred people) attended his events around the country. Students attended intimate intensives held around the pool at JZ's ranch in Yelm, Washington. Her autobiography, published in 1987, coincided with the spread of her work to Europe and Australia.

Australians responded enthusiastically to Ramtha's books and tapes, which had been released there since 1986. And in early November 1987, JZ held a dialogue in Sydney, the first intensive held outside the United States. Because Australia's New Age community had warmly embraced Ramtha's teachings,

JZ's coming was a time of great celebration. At the intensive, Ramtha shared an overview of his perspective and then centered on the liberation and empowerment of women.[25] (JZ returned to Australia in October 1989 and January 1990, also stopping for events in Auckland, New Zealand.)

JZ made her first appearance in England in November 1988 and appeared in Munich in December 1989. In England, Gita Bellin, as Ramtha's representative in both the United Kingdom and throughout the British Commonwealth, established an organization, the Friends of Ramtha, and throughout 1988 sponsored events in London and Glastonbury (one of the major centers of New Age interest in England) at which videos were shown and questions answered. Bellin's efforts pioneered Ramtha's permeation throughout Europe's sizable New Age community. Ramtha's books were translated into German, Dutch, French, Norwegian, Spanish, and Italian.

70

THE GOAL OF THE WORK: RAMTHA'S SCHOOL

By the end of 1987, JZ probably realized that all the activity of her first ten years with Ramtha was leading toward starting a school. The decade had served many purposes. It had allowed her time to accommodate to Ramtha using her body, to gain confidence in him and what he was doing through her. And it had allowed Ramtha to become known. By 1987, however, a special group had emerged who were ready for a more serious level of encounter.

Several hundred more involved students gathered on May 13–15, 1988, during which time Ramtha lectured on what he was about to launch.[26] Then, during the week of May 22–28, 1988, more than five hundred people attended a retreat at Snow Mountain in Colorado, at which time Ramtha's School of Enlightenment was formally launched. During that week the basic philosophy and practice that now dominate the school were brought together for the first time. In 1988 a new era began.

Meanwhile, JZ needed more space in Yelm to accommodate people who lived in the area and wanted to receive Ramtha's advanced teachings. A large arena for exercising and showing horses had been constructed on the ranch. It could now be refurbished as an assembly hall for students, and events could easily be shifted from JZ's home to the hall.

Two events made the shift to the hall permanent. In November 1988, JZ and those who staffed the Ramtha Dialogues arrived in New York City and discovered that the people with whom they had dealt were gone. The new staff had canceled all the arrangements and had instead erected a tent in an adjacent lot. Infuriated, JZ canceled the event and refunded everyone's fees. Then, four months later a major, two-week-long event was scheduled for eleven hundred people, again at Snow Mountain in Colorado. Soon after the event opened, the staff began receiving threatening phone calls that culminated in a bomb threat. JZ canceled the rest of the event and soon afterward decided to abandon any further public appearances except for a few overseas. This decision was reinforced by the increasing demands upon JZ's time.

Thus by the summer of 1989, all of the elements so familiar to Ramtha's School as it is today were essentially in place. With the problems of founding the school removed, JZ could face the 1990s with some degree of confidence.

71

$\sim$

5

RAMTHA'S
PHILOSOPHY

B ut before a school could begin, some basic underlying concepts were needed. Like most teachers who operate outside
the dominant Western theistic tradition, Ramtha denounces
mere ideas; they can do only so much, and too frequently they
can, at their worst, make one adhere to them for their own sake,
whether or not they have a function in one's life. For example,
many Christians hold to a statement of beliefs, such as the idea
of the Trinity, because they have been told it is the correct understanding of God even though they have no conception of its
importance in theology and its role in shaping their individual
piety. "Truth is only truth," asserts Ramtha, "when it is relevant
to personal growth."[1]

A NEW WORLDVIEW

Ramtha holds great respect for cognition as a necessary step to
gaining a new understanding of the self. So entrapped are individuals in the dominant worldview, a worldview that denies to
individuals their powers as creative gods, he says, that some philosophical basis must be given to help students reorient their
thinking patterns so they can eventually accept changes produced

by practicing his spiritual disciplines. Average "limited" people cannot believe they possess the powers to manifest. New Agers readily affirm "I am god," but Ramtha notes how their actions betray their lack of faith. They possess no experiential base to go beyond and really trust their lives to act as if they are gods and in possession of godlike powers. They may be on their way to becoming mystics but hardly masters. Ramtha explained the problem to one god entity who had become a student:

> Life upon life, existence upon existence, you became so immersed in the illusions of this plane that you forgot the wonderful fire that flows through you. In ten and one-half million years you have come from being sovereign and all-powerful entities, to where you are utterly lost in matter; enslaved by your own creations of dogma, law, fashion, and tradition; separated by country, creed, sex, and race; immersed in jealousy, bitterness, guilt, and fear. You so identified yourselves with your bodies that you entrapped yourselves in survival and forgot the unseen essence that you truly are—that God within you allows you to create your dreams however you choose. Immortality you have openly rejected; and for that, you will die . . . and return here, again and again and again. Thus, here you are again, after ten and one-half million years of living here . . . and you hang on to your disbeliefs.[2]

74

The new philosophy is also acting upon tradition. Just as Theosophy moved the Gnostic teachings into a post-Newtonian and post-Darwinian world, so Ramtha is moving his students into a post-Einsteinian, post-quantum world. The teaching of quantum physics is quickly overturning our worldview as we become aware of the lack of "substance" in matter, of energy compressed and configured in space, and of the fragility of perception so forcefully presented in virtual reality games. We have also lost our feeling of *terra firma* and now see Earth as floating through the endless realms of space.

Most of us live and function quite successfully with the commonsense philosophy of the nineteenth century. Matter, in spite of what physicists have demonstrated, seems quite solid. In spite of the images of *Star Trek*, we still struggle to claim our little plots of land upon which to build our homes. Our ordinary potential can still take us most of the way up the social ladder. For some of us, however, the commonsense world has not worked, but it's the only world we know. If we are to get out of our situations, we have to get out of that world. And essential to change is a change of philosophy. A new worldview will not do it by itself, but without it, the change is impossible.

Although many students have read the White Book, the basic text of the movement, few are prepared for their sink-or-swim immersion in the new worldview, which occurs during the first weekend at Ramtha's school. And they listen diligently. Periodically Ramtha pauses and asks students to relate to their neighbors what he has just said. Still, almost no one walks away with more than an outline of Ramtha's views. Advanced students are encouraged to repeat basic events and listen again to the beginning lectures in light of their ongoing experiences. They understand more and more each time they revisit the metaphysical material. Ramtha also continually shifts the presentation, presenting the basic teachings from a slightly different angle, attempting to communicate with different students coming from different backgrounds.

THE FORMATION OF THE UNIVERSE

Ramtha's transformed Gnosticism begins, as do many Gnostic systems, with the beginning, and in the beginning was the Void (God with a capital G). The Void is best understood as a sea of potentiality. In presenting this concept, Ramtha asks students to repeat the answer to a basic question, Who or what is God? "One vast nothing materially, all things potentially!" God is no-thing. God is not life, God is the giver of life. God is no "thing," but the potential from which all things can exist.[3] There is no time. There is no space. There is no-thing.

At some point in an eternal (timeless), mythological past, the Void turned in upon itself and contemplated (became aware of) itself. Contemplation of the Void created Consciousness, and Consciousness is inextricably combined with Energy: Consciousness is a thought, Energy is the active ingredient of that thought. Together they produce an idea, awareness. As a result of the contemplation, there appeared in the Void a point of awareness, mythologically the child of God (product of the Void), most frequently referred to as Point Zero. Point Zero possessed momentum, an important attribute.

The Void impressed upon Point Zero a creative thought: "Make of me what you will. Make known the unknown! Allow me (the Void) to know what I am."

That primordial awareness, that dot (remembering from geometry that a dot has no dimensions) in the Void, turned in upon itself and contemplated itself. As a result, a second thought, another point of awareness, a secondary entity, was created. Actually, numerous new points of awareness appeared simultaneously, and each individual who now exists was one of those points of awareness. Between Point Zero and the secondary point(s) there existed a flux, an energized atmosphere; in there time and space appeared.

A place emerged in the sea of the Void. It filled with particums of energy, protoparticles that emerged from and were the products of the pulling away of two levels. (In Ramtha's system, as in other Gnostic systems, seven levels of awareness were generated. The primordial Point Zero exists at the top of the seventh level. This is also termed the seventh heaven.)[4] These entities lived in the new atmosphere, which was filled with ultra-frequency energy. This energy is analogous to the particles of sub-atomic physics, those mysterious particles that seem to behave exactly as the observer expects them to behave. They are in part controlled by the thoughts of the Observer (the entity).

THE SEVEN LEVELS OF THE UNIVERSE

The seven levels of the universe are reflected in numerous realities; some form an important part of Ramtha's teachings. The most important correlates, including the seven seals in the human body discussed later in this chapter, are listed in Table 1.

As mentioned in Ramtha's system, seven levels were generated. Because of their relatively close proximity to Point Zero and the seventh level, entities at the sixth level vibrated at an exceedingly hyper-frequency energy. And as entities thought and experienced, they created by their thoughts one possible world out of the potentiality of the Void. The building blocks of that world were the minute particums of energy that emerged out of the momentum of the Void. These particums also vibrated at the high-frequency level at which the entities existed. Because time is relative to frequency, time also moved exceedingly fast in that world. As entities thought, they created, which impressed form upon the particums of energy. And as they created, they experienced. That repeated gestalt of thought-creation-experience is what is termed *mind*. Mind is the major product of life in the levels of existence. But there was also the urge to know more.

An important lesson emerges from discussion of the sixth level. To create is to think; thinking makes it so. Although other steps may be involved, especially at the lower levels, at any level the beginning thought is the important creative moment necessary to bring any reality into being.

The process of exploring more of the Void, the potential, began with a refocus on Point Zero. In refocusing, the entities in effect returned to it and then moved out further. In doing so they brought into existence the fifth level. The distance between the entities and Point Zero created a new atmosphere characterized

77

Table 1. The Seven Levels Correlated

Level	Electro-magnetic Spectrum	Consciousness	Human Body	Embodiment
7	Infinite Unknown	Ultraconsciousness	Pituitary gland	Point Zero
6	Gamma ray	Hyperconsciousness	Pineal gland	Energy body
5	X ray	Superconsciousness	Thyroid gland	Golden body
4	Ultraviolet	Bridge consciousness	Thymus	Blue body
3	Visible light	Awareness	Solar plexus	Light body
2	Infrared	Social consciousness	Sacral plexus	Astral body
1	Hertizan	Subconsciousness	Reproductive organs	Physical body

by a slowing of frequency. Here time was still very fast, but slower relative to the sixth level.

The building blocks of the fifth level were those particums of energy slowed from the sixth level. Here, by drawing upon the knowledge of the sixth level and the possibilities of the new, fifth level, a new world was created. Each entity created an energy body that vibrated in accordance with its new level. Each grew a new mind by its creative activity.

Characteristic of the fifth level is a golden radiant hue because of the slowing of energy particles while they moved from the sixth level. When a frequency is slowed, it decays. When it decays it gives off radiation, and on this level it was seen as a golden hue. Each level is distinct from all others in a way analogous to the levels at which electrons exist as they absorb and give off quanta of energy.

Entities again felt compelled to explore other aspects of the Void, to make known the unknown. To establish the fourth level, entities again focused upon Point Zero, returned to it, and then moved into an area where time and vibration were slower. In the process they left behind their golden bodies and slowed their rate of vibration.

The fourth level is suffused with a bluish light, again from the radiating decay of particles from the fifth level. This level is the ultraviolet world, beautiful yet slower than the golden realm of the fifth level. Here entities took on blue bodies. Here also, with the knowledge carried from the higher levels and with the potentialities of the new level, they created a new world appropriate to the frequency at which they lived.

Ramtha emphasizes two ideas. First, all living humans passed through the seventh, sixth, fifth, and fourth levels. They all possessed the bodies relative to the levels they left behind, which are waiting for them when they return or when they wish to use them. Second, the sixth-level energy body had no shape and the fifth-level golden body took on the outline, if none of the peculiar aspects, of the present physical body. The fourth-level blue body, however, was recognizably human but androgynous. It had the potential for being male or female.

At the fourth level a choice was made. Some entities found the fourth level so beautiful and satisfying that they chose to stay. Others decided to continue the exploration process by descending to the third level, the realm of visible light.

THE BIG BANG

The movements through levels to the fourth level had been relatively smooth transitions. The next step to the third level, itself a matter of contention among the fourth-level dwellers, became a traumatic, explosive event. Those who chose to go on did so. They gathered at the border of the ultraviolet level and made their descent to the next level. As they moved, the event triggered what is known as the big bang. The particles that were pulled through the curtain dividing the fourth and third levels erupted and split into polar opposites, negative and positive, darkness and light, magnetic push and pull. Even time itself split.

The third level is the realm of light, and the entities who passed into this realm assumed beautiful if relatively slow-vibrating (in relation to the fourth level) light bodies, whose particles vibrated at the frequency range of visible light. These brilliant, shining, noncorporeal bodies were proper for a world created from light.

Light bodies are described frequently by people who have had near-death experiences and report meeting entities of light. Many accounts describe such events in a traditional Christian context and even ascribe Christlike characteristics to the light body that was met as consciousness slipped out of the physical body and moved to the arena of light beings. However, Ramtha insists that those who have near-death experiences encounter the exalted beings of their own light bodies.[5]

When entities moved to the second level, they assumed bodies and created a world at the infrared rate of vibration. This realm is what in nineteenth-century Spiritualist and older esoteric literature is termed the astral realm or the shadowland. It represents a slowing of light and may best be thought of as the negative image of the light realm. It is the realm of the psychic, where psychic or extrasensory communication (ESP) occurs. The bodies in this realm resemble shadows (the traditional ghosts). The second level is also the realm of earthbound entities. Humans, after death, can find the astral a frightful realm to reencounter.[6]

The final descent to the first level was made as entities moved into the slowest realm of gross matter, described as coagulation. Energy coagulates into what we know as matter. As entities began life on the material level, so human history (or, rather, prehistory) began.

THE LIFE OF THE GODS BECOMING

The process by which the gods moved into bodies somewhat like the ones we possess today had three key creative phases. First, the gods created bodies for themselves that were primitively androgynous. If a new body replacement was desired, it could be produced by cloning, because each cell (in the DNA) carried the pattern of the whole. However, this process did not allow for novelty. Therefore, in the second phase cloning was abandoned and the gods learned to create new bodies by thought. They dreamed bodies and coagulated them from the "clay of the earth"—the energy particles of the world. They then turned to their task of making known the unknown and building a world out of the images they dreamed. They created a blueprint to which the world would conform; in biblical terms, Adam named the creatures of the Garden of Eden. So, not only could gods dream bodies, but also they could "dream" objects, and the objects would be manifest.[7] The world as we know it, the flora and fauna, derived from the dreams of the gods through the millennia. The creativity of the dreams, however, also reached a point of exhaustion, and the process of image-making became repetitive.

81

In the third phase, the entities perceived that life around them, especially animal life, was bipolar—it had gender. Hence they envisioned a new body, the dual self. But the process of bringing a new creation into existence involved more than the simple coagulation of particles into gross-matter existence. It required a radical movement back to the fourth level.

When the entities returned to the fourth level, they brought with them all the experiences of life in the first, second, and third levels. At the fourth level, and with the potential of their blue bodies, they began to create the image of bodies with gender. (The blue body is genderless, but carries the potential for gender.) Some decided to be male (positive in the electrical sense) and others to be female (negative in the electrical sense). Neither the consciousness nor the blue body took on gender identification, but as the entities returned to the third level, their light bodies immediately assumed either a male or female identification, and in the second realm their astral bodies took on sexual polarity. When the entities returned to their gross bodies in the first realm and awoke from their sleep, some "were as Adam with male sexual organs and some were as Eve, with the peculiarly female organ."[8] This return occurred some ten and one-half million years ago.

Thus new possibilities became available, including sharing with each other sexually and creating children. The children could embody the intense ideas for alteration their parents had dreamed. The creative process of making known the unknown could continue.

When the gods awoke in their new bodies they faced a somewhat neutral environment. Earth was enclosed in a fog through which the sun shown, but its light was diffused. Their bodies, very different from those we inhabit today, were hairy, their arms were longer, they could move on all fours, and their fingers and toes were adapted for climbing. Anthropologists gave the name *Homo erectus* to these new humans. Here Ramtha makes a credible alignment with biological evolution developed by geologists and anthropologists.

Ramtha emphasizes that human incarnation was not intended to last forever. It was a game to be experienced and enjoyed, a new adventure in exploration of the unknown. But some people have lived as many as 30,000 incarnated existences.

As Ramtha unfolds this revised Gnostic myth, students begin to grasp the rationale behind the many assertions in the early dialogues and begin to construct new self-images. They understand that they are the primal creations of the Void, not the end products. They realize that neither were they put here by a capricious deity nor did they merely evolve accidentally; they chose to come here for the experience of life in gross matter. They are not supposed to be, nor do they have to be, mere passive reactors to outside forces (be they physical, biological, or psychological). They are supposed to be the creative active force in the world. They are sleepy, lazy masters who have forgotten, and they have denied their purpose, powers, and abilities. Within their subconscious lies all the levels of reality about which most are only vaguely aware. By tapping into those realities, Ramtha asserts, they can regain their lost status.

83

DEATH AND BEYOND

People commonly are inquisitive about death. Do we survive, and if so, in what form? Do we go on to a heavenly existence, or do we reincarnate? Ramtha has spoken clearly on these issues in terms that would be familiar to a Spiritualist or Theosophist, though less so to a traditional Christian. In Ramtha's cosmology, when we die we immediately confront the astral world. Our astral bodies are mirror images of our physical bodies. According to those who have seen such astral bodies (and seeing people who have recently died in their astral bodies—as ghosts—is a commonly reported experience), they can at times appear as substantive and as real as physical bodies; at other times they seem somewhat vague and ghostlike. Bible translator J. B. Phillips, for example, tells of his experience with author-theologian C. S. Lewis, whom Phillips did not know well and had seen only once in person.

> A few days after his [Lewis's] death while I was watching television, he "appeared" to me, and spoke a few words which were particularly relevant to the difficult circumstance through which I was passing. He was ruddier in complexion than ever, grinning all over his face, and as the old-fashioned saying has it, positively glowing with health.[9]

Astral bodies can on occasion be picked up on film. People have reported seeing the astral body float away from the physical body as it disengages at the moment of death. For some, ignorant of the afterlife, the astral world provides a familiar existence. On occasion, if Spiritualist stories are to be believed, people may not even realize they are dead. They may walk around their homes and workplaces as if they were still alive, only to slowly realize and accept their condition when they realize they're unable to communicate or pick up objects.

Spiritualist literature has numerous accounts explaining hauntings as the result of people who are emotionally bound to physical existence and are unable or unwilling to go on until their unfinished business is resolved. Ramtha agrees that being stuck in the astral is an unhappy and unnatural state.

Normally, upon death we move to the light (third) realm. This realm is equivalent to the Summerland of nineteenth-century Spiritualism and the Christian heaven. Here we encounter our light bodies and our consciousnesses reassume possession of them. Knowledge of our immediate past life is lost. Nor do we remember our past incarnations, because knowledge of them has been stripped away. All that remains are the bottom-line lessons of experience, ingrained traits, and habit patterns. The wisdom we have gained (or the ignorance assumed) returns with us into a new incarnation and surfaces as otherwise individual characteristics that mix with information passed through the DNA of our parents.

Our present light bodies also mirror our present physical bodies; hence, the opportunity for change in the next incarnation is extremely limited. Only those very few events that strongly impress us and lead to a significant alteration of personality will be brought to a new incarnation.

Ramtha also notes that over thousands of incarnations each person alive today has lived a wide range of human experience. We have lived what we may think of as very good lives and very bad ones; we have loved and hated, victimized others and been victimized by others, slain and been slain. What has been called karma by others operates to some extent but is by no means the universal "legal" principle in which many New Agers trust. For Ramtha, we live in a universe in which morality is necessary for human existence, facilitating the work of the gods in their primary duty to make known the unknown. In light of the eternal existence of the self, the particularities of human culture and social interaction are of relative importance only, not relevant to ultimate concerns.

ACCESSING THE LEVELS

Primitive humans, who still remembered their origin and purpose upon entering physical existence, could access all levels through which they had passed. Today, even in our forgetful state, we can easily access what Ramtha terms the astral plane, and all of us regularly do it if only during sleep while dreaming or when we act upon our intuition. Access to the light (third) plane is also relatively easy. Many of us have experienced it, if only at odd moments (such as those who have gone through near-death or other kinds of visionary experiences).[10]

Ramtha teaches students the means of consciously accessing the levels. These means form the substance of the school and function for the students in much the same manner that pietistic practices function for church members. For example, as a young Christian, I was taught the importance of showing Christian love to others, reading and understanding the Bible, daily prayer, and regular church attendance, along with many lesser instructions. For a member of a metaphysical or Gnostic group, other things are important, but generally at the top of the list is something called demonstration or manifestation. As access is opened to the spiritual world, great value is placed upon demonstrating that one has gained access and then is manifesting mastery over aspects of that world.[11]

In Ramtha's School of Enlightenment, understanding the inner structure of the world and the evolution of humans is a first step in gaining access to and some control over the levels. The most important aspect, however, is the practice of spiritual disciplines (discussed in chapter 6). Ramtha's philosophy both informs students on what will be occurring and offers direction on what they should be attempting to accomplish as they engage in the disciplines. And because the idea informs the action, so the action makes the ideas clear, understandable, and acceptable.

The Gnostic system is new to all the students, and the assumption is made that at the beginning no one really believes it because it flies in the face of so much Western-style common-sense philosophy. However, as students have astral-, light-, and blue-body experiences, each possessing qualitative differences, the rationale of the philosophy becomes more comprehensible and living it more acceptable. Here advanced students often sit through the beginning workshops again, during which they report understanding teachings they'd completely missed before.

Understanding the relationship that the students perceive between Ramtha's philosophical teachings and their experience of spiritual disciplines requires understanding how most Christian churches view theological affirmations versus how Gnostic groups view belief systems. Most churches derive beliefs from the Bible and use a creedal-like statement summarizing the major teachings of the Bible, which itself is somewhat thought of as a revelation from God. Young Christians are asked to affirm those beliefs and to begin to base their behavior upon them. If all goes well, the truth of some of those beliefs is later confirmed through life experience. However, some beliefs concern matters that can be confirmed only in the afterlife, and ascent to those truths is generally expected, even though they cannot be experienced.

In Gnostic groups, truth is immediately and directly tied to the experience of confirming events. Theosophy, for example, frequently uses the phrase "There is no religion higher than truth." Theosophical groups present a precise view of the world. They also circulate literature and sponsor speakers offering many variations on that worldview. One does not have to accept their teachings to become a member. However, the leadership is confident that those who continue their study of Theosophy will come to accept their teachings as true. In like measure, Ramtha presents a definite picture of the world, not totally unlike Theosophy (but nevertheless differing at several key points). Acceptance of the teachings is not demanded; after all, they are only philosophy, which may be useful in interpreting the experiences that come out of the practice. However, as one continues in the practice, experiences will confirm the "truth" of the teachings. Together, teachings and experiences become a total package to be accepted or rejected at a later date.

DYNAMICS OF THE BRAIN

Ramtha demonstrates a healthy respect for the body in general and the brain in particular, a respect largely absent in the Gnostic tradition, which has tended to denigrate the material (including the body) in favor of a complete focus upon the spiritual. Ramtha, however, considers the brain a magnificent product of evolution and proper understanding of its functioning a necessary element toward enlightenment. And ultimately, the physical body can become immortal when it becomes the habitation of an awakened conscious self. On the physical plane, however, bodies are the gods' proper vehicles for their present missions.

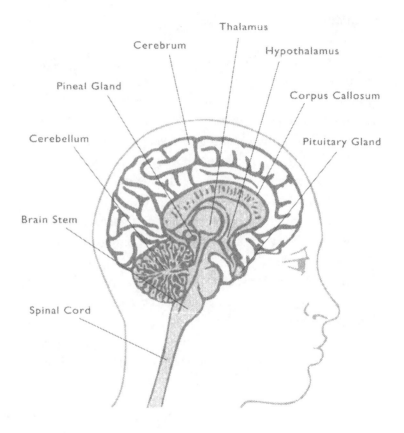

Thalamus

Cerebrum

Hypothalamus

Pineal Gland

Corpus Callosum

Cerebellum

Pituitary Gland

Brain Stem

Spinal Cord

Figure 1. The Brain

The brain structure is generally divided into three sections: the *reptilian*, which includes the cerebellum and lower brain stem; the *midbrain*, which includes the upper brain stem; and the *forebrain*, which includes the thalamus, hypothalamus, pituitary gland, pineal gland, corpus callosum, and the large modern cerebrum (see figure 1). The brain stem grades into the spinal column and the body's peripheral nervous system. Although much about the brain remains unknown, certain parts do handle various functions. For example, balance and coordination are regulated in the cerebellum. The brains stem houses control centers for the digestive, respiratory, and circulatory systems. The hypothalamus coordinates the two systems for sending instructions to your body: the nervous system (electrical) and the endocrine system (chemical). The thalamus sorts and relays sensory impulses to the cerebrum. The cerebrum controls voluntary motor functions; processes sensory data coming in from the eyes, ears, nose, mouth, and skin; and stores memory. Thinking—the intellectual processing of ideas—also occurs in the cerebrum. The pituitary and pineal gland are often thought to be the seat of psychic abilities. Some esoteric teachers correlate the pineal gland with what is termed the third eye, the area of ESP.

89

The important part of brain and body function for Ramtha's students concerns the way in which dreaming occurs and imaging takes place. The Great Work—doing magic, becoming a creator in the world—begins by learning to create images in the brain, holding those images in consciousness, and allowing the consciousness to manifest them.

Understanding of the brain begins by discussing the primitive brain of Homo erectus, because one goal of the school is to recover some abilities of Homo erectus that have been pushed aside as the cerebrum developed and became the dominant part of the brain. In Homo erectus the cerebellum received sensory data as frequency impulses and turned them into mental images. The cerebellum could also store that data for future reference. Thus, having once seen and heard a whippoorwill make its unique call, Homo erectus could recall that image and sound quite apart from seeing or hearing it again. The pineal gland and the thalamus received information psychically, apart from the senses, and directly from the environment through thought. These data were communicated to the cerebellum, which then transformed them into images and pictures. Finally, through the pineal gland *Homo erectus* could also communicate intuitively with other entities, both animate and inanimate.

The cerebellum, the brain stem, and the glands served as a throne supporting that part of the brain seen as the most sacred part of the body: the front of the forebrain (then the corpus callosum, now the cerebrum). This is the area most people in Spiritualist, metaphysical, and New Age circles term the third eye. If you close your eyes and imagine you are looking at a movie screen inside your head, you seem to be looking at your forehead above your nose. Here pictures occur as you meditate or fantasize. Whatever is established in this space is what Ramtha refers to as a dream. Images in the frontal lobe will be realized in the outer world.

Homo erectus understood the power of the dream, the image held in consciousness at the frontal lobe. *Homo erectus* would focus upon that image, go to sleep, and awake to find manifested what had been dreamed. These early humans knew that they were gods on a mission to make known the unknown. They did not know the future, which existed only as potential. But they had a conscious connection upward through the levels to Point Zero.[12]

Whatever rests in the forehead, the entire organism experiences as a dream through the action of the nervous system. We do not understand that fact, asserts Ramtha. Rather than willfully placing images in the frontal lobe, we passively receive images from the culture, and those images constitute reality for us. We force a reality upon ourselves rather than become the creators of what will be.

Ramtha, by using his spiritual disciplines, now assumes a herculean task: to reverse the effects of years of mental passivity and turn students into creators who can mold and shape reality, who have the ability to understand and continue the initial prime directive, Make known the unknown.

Top: Ramtha's students engage in fieldwork. *Bottom left:* A student focuses during fieldwork. *Bottom right:* After fieldwork, a student proudly wears the cards she has found.

Top left: JZ Knight. *Top right:* JZ Knight while channeling Ramtha. *Bottom:* Scientists wire JZ Knight as she prepares to channel Ramtha.

6

PRACTICES FOR
SPIRITUAL FORMATION

The first time I visited Ramtha's School of Enlightenment, I saw students engaged in a most unusual activity. They were in a large field surrounded by a chest-high fence walking around blindfolded. I was informed that there was a method to this madness. The students were searching for index-type cards they had made earlier in the day that had been placed face down on the fence. Invited to join the fray, I made a card upon which I drew a picture of something I greatly desired. With the loan of a blindfold and some rudimentary instructions about getting used to the field, I launched forth with conflicting feelings of never being able to find my card amid several hundred others and a confidence that if anyone could do it, I could. Shortly after I entered the field, someone called out that she had found her card; after that every few minutes (it soon became hard to judge time) someone else whooped and hollered. My confidence soared even as the calculation of the odds against finding my card filled my head.

Then another thought arose: "By the way, where is the fence?" I had been in the field for some time and had yet to find my way to the edge. When I finally reached the railing, I had crossed a small ditch and was at the other end of the field.

After I became somewhat comfortable with the physical space and with learning to walk in straight lines rather than in circles, additional horrors emerged. Although Yelm is in the quiet country-side of the state of Washington, I quickly became aware of numerous distractions, from passing trucks to the occasional airplane. The primary distraction, however, was all the other people: After staying in the field for a little while, the demand to succeed arises. Other people find their cards. A few find multiple cards. Why can't I? Then there is the temptation to forget the purpose of the exercise and to find the card no matter what the cost. Occasional admonishments concerning cheating are given until this phase is passed.

Needless to say, though I diligently pursued it for several hours, I did not find my card. However, the time was not lost. In this initial period and during subsequent periods, I learned a good deal about the kinds of subtle pressures this exercise puts on people. During conversations with students, all talked of having to deal with essentially the same problems.

The real questions about what seemed at first glance a meaningless game of hide-and-seek were, How does it fit into the training program? What, if anything, does it have to do with spirituality? How could searching for a card become a step in shaping spiritual life? The only practice it called to my mind was the meditative walking of Zen Buddhists, but that was stretching for an analogy.

After leaving the field and regrouping in the assembly hall, Ramtha and the students honored those who had found their cards. But why was finding one's card such a cause for celebration? All these questions have answers, but to answer them requires a broader perspective on the program of spiritual formation, the gestalt of outward activity students undertake to gain familiarity with the inner self.

CONSCIOUSNESS AND ENERGY

From Ramtha's philosophy, which forms the school's intellectual basis, a core idea emerged. Consciousness and Energy are the essential realities of the universe. Energized consciousness creates reality. Therefore, a focused and energized consciousness can *re-create* an individual's world. Drawing upon an understanding of the manner in which thoughts lead to the shaping of reality, Ramtha claims to be able to train students to hold ideas in consciousness and eventually manifest them. The method is termed Consciousness & Energy (C&E), or concentrated dreaming combined with an intense breathing. C&E is the heart of the information offered to beginning students and is the foundation upon which all other spiritual disciplines are constructed.

The practice of C&E is best understood in light of what Ramtha calls the *seven seals*, the seven universal levels manifesting in the body. Some will recognize the similarity between the seals and *chakras*. Chakras are viewed as the sense organs of the etheric body (or human double) and serve as the connecting link between the physical body and its incorporeal etheric double. Through them the physical body is supplied with necessary vitality. Chakra, a Sanskrit word meaning disk or wheel, is frequently pictured as either a spinning vortex of energy or an unfolding lotus flower. Five of the seven chakras are located on points along the spine from its base to the area behind the throat. The last two are at the forehead and the top or crown of the skull (see figure 2).

In theosophical teachings, the chakras are also associated in the physical body both with the nervous system (in areas with collections of nerve cells serving particular parts of the body) and with the endocrine glands, which secrete hormones directly into the bloodstream. Together the nervous system and the endocrine glands coordinate and integrate the individual's response to stimuli, both received from the outside and generated from within. To Ramtha, the concept of chakras includes the idea of energy crossings. These crossings create a grid system; in fact, the whole body is made up of an energy grid resembling something like a giant web. Thus, every energy crossing would be a chakra and all main crossing points major chakras.[1]

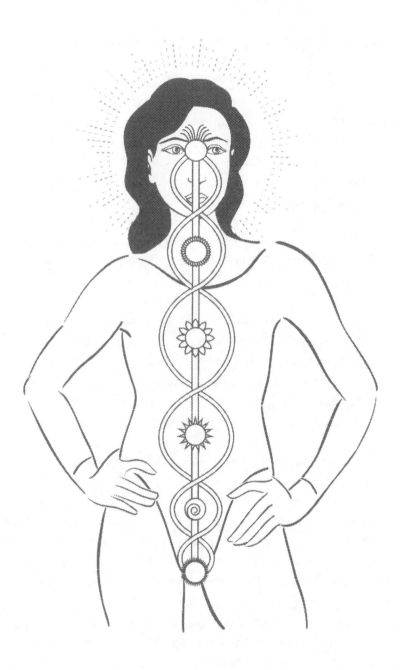

Figure 2. The Chakras As Traditionally Presented

Ramtha replaces the idea of chakras with that of seals, points on the body associated with the nerve ganglia and the endocrine glands and their hormone secretions. (For a comparison of chakras and seals, see table 2.) He uses the metaphor of a hot wax seal placed upon a closed document and notes that a broken seal means someone has tampered with the document. In the body, a seal is a place where energy is most potent, and when opened the energy freely pours forth.

In average humans, the first three seals are already open. These seals dominate important areas of our lives and correspond to the primary issues of propagation or sexuality (first seal), pain or survival (second seal), and power (third seal), especially social power (see figure 3). They radiate an energy that constructs (and constricts) individual reality. If one's energy radiates primarily from one seal, that energy will largely determine one's construction of reality. It becomes proper, then, to speak of certain personality types being produced by the location of the energy they are sending outward. Thus we can speak of people whose identity is located at the first seal as being sexual beings, whose very presence exudes sensuality and whose minds are oriented toward sexual arousal and culmination. Sexual issues in these people dominate the images in their frontal lobes. Such people are magnetic and attract people by their very presence.

Some people suffer to the point of hypochondria. Their identities are built around the second seal (pain). Bodily disorder images predominate in their frontal lobes, and their worlds revolve around issues raised by their suffering. Those who live from the third seal (power) will be weak individuals—victims continually manipulated by other or, the flip side of the victim, the victimizer, the dominant personality who always manipulates others.

In most people, the fourth seal (and all higher seals) is closed. It is associated with the thymus gland, which, according to Ramtha, has been degenerating since puberty. If the thymus could be revived, it would be a fountain of youth. As the fourth seal is opened, spiritual transformation begins. Ultimately, the

Table 2. The Seven Chakras and Seven Seals Compared

Chakra	Location	Nerve Ganglia	Endocrines	Seven Seals Location	Body Correlates
7th	Top of head	Cerebral cortex	Pituitary	Forehead	Pituitary gland
6th	Forehead	Carotid plexus	Pineal	Midskull	Pineal grand
5th	Throat	Pharyngeal plexus	Thyroid, parathyroid	Throat	Thyroid gland
4th	Heart	Pulmonary and cardiac plexi	Thymus	Midchest	Thymus
3rd	Solar plexus	Solar plexus	Adrenals, pancreas	Abdomen	Solar plexus
2nd	Lower abdomen	Sacral plexus	Ovaries, testicles	Lower abdomen	Sacral plexus
1st	Base of spine	Coccygeal plexus	Adrenals	Genital area	Testicles, ovaries

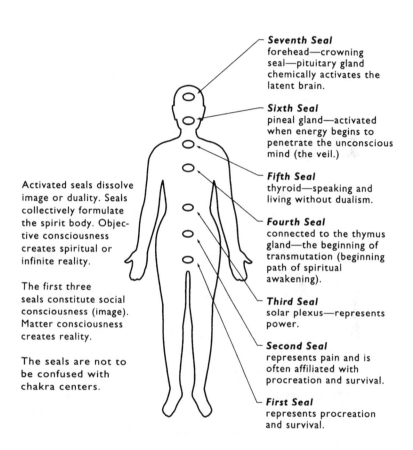

Seventh Seal
forehead—crowning
seal—pituitary gland
chemically activates the
latent brain.

Sixth Seal
pineal gland—activated
when energy begins to
penetrate the unconscious
mind (the veil.)

Fifth Seal
thyroid—speaking and
living without dualism.

Fourth Seal
connected to the thymus
gland—the beginning of
transmutation (beginning
path of spiritual
awakening).

Third Seal
solar plexus—represents
power.

Second Seal
represents pain and is
often affiliated with
procreation and survival.

First Seal
represents procreation
and survival.

Activated seals dissolve
image or duality. Seals
collectively formulate
the spirit body. Objec-
tive consciousness
creates spiritual or
infinite reality.

The first three
seals constitute social
consciousness (image).
Matter consciousness
creates reality.

The seals are not to
be confused with
chakra centers.

Figure 3. The Seals According to Ramtha

Great Work (that is, real magic) is about opening the four upper seals and learning to operate (to construct reality) at the seventh seal, a task easier alluded to in the abstract than in comprehending or experiencing. In fact, comprehending the work of the upper-level seals and experiencing it cannot be separated.

PRACTICING C&E

Armed with some idea of the seven seals, students are almost ready to begin C&E, but first Ramtha supplies one additional item crucial to operating the seals. Behind the first seal, most often associated with the reproductive organs, sits a reservoir of energy, the *kundalini*. In traditional Hindu lore the kundalini is seen as a latent force in the human body, pictured generally as a serpent lying coiled at the base of the spine. When aroused, the energy travels up the spine, often accompanied by feelings of heat, pain, or electricity. When it reaches the top of the head (the crown chakra in tantric thought), it unfolds like a cobra and brings enlightenment.[2]

Ramtha teaches the basic discipline of the breath, by which students can begin to access kundalini energy and bring it to their frontal lobes. Instructing students requires Ramtha, a master teacher, to administer it properly. Ramtha calls himself a hierophant: one who has the power not only to instruct a discipline but to initiate students into greater experience and personal truth.

Practicing C&E consciously moves energy to the brain. The work is thus done within, but not passively, nor is there movement into a trance state. Mystical enlightenment, in a Hindu sense, is not the goal so much as is empowering individuals to re-create their worlds, the ultimate goal being mastership. As students' skills develop, their conscious will predominates.[3]

A straight spine, unsupported by a backrest, is emphasized early. It facilitates the movement of energy and is a first step in mastering the body. As training progresses, the exercise radically extends the students' comfort zones.

The breathing technique is combined with practical work on self-change. Beginning students list traits they would like to change or items they would like to have. They then choose a word to represent each item on their wish lists and focus upon one of those words, holding it in their minds' eye or, as Ramtha frequently reminds them, in their frontal lobes. After students feel comfortable focusing on their words, they hold the words in their consciousnesses while doing the breathing exercise. Then, having entered an altered state, students drive their words into their subconscious and manifestation can begin. After the exercise students relax and allow their subconscious to accept and initiate work on the wishes received.

Mastering the primary C&E technique is important because all other work in the school is based upon it. The practice will evolve within each student, but as the basics are mastered and become second nature, the essence of the initial C&E exercise remains constant.

101

Students are told to expect positive changes in their lives, especially in improved health and living conditions, from the first C&E practice. Such changes do occur, and in many cases those changes are what bring students back for further instruction. Ramtha suggests that C&E actually changes body chemistry and produces a more healthful condition at a basic level. Most notable are the raised blood levels of protein and brain chemicals, which improve the body by overwhelming its normally acid base environment.

USING C&E

For average students, C&E is, in the beginning, hard work. They do it because Ramtha prods them with the prize of accomplishment and because he assures them that C&E will quickly become second nature. In this respect beginning C&E stands in sharp contrast to many practices that follow, in that practices possess an element of play that makes them "fun," especially in their initial stages, which creates a recreational atmosphere while students work on their school assignments.

The element of play is not mere happenstance but crucial to the success of the curriculum. For example, one early practice is termed "sending and receiving," with additional designations such as "remote viewing" given to its variations. Sending and receiving is basic training for most psychic-development groups, and most people involved in metaphysical teachings have seen other groups engaged in a similar practice. At the school, the practice differs primarily in that it is embedded in C&E and is done in a group of several hundred people. These are not superficial differences.

Ramtha divides two hundred or more students into two groups and assigns each person in Group A to a partner in Group B. He then puts them to the test, though the atmosphere is one of playing a game. Each Group A student thinks of an object and draws it on a sheet of paper. Group A students then do C&E, only this time they focus upon the pictures they have drawn—they hold the images of those pictures in their frontal lobes. Thus they are practicing the willful selection of an object to hold in consciousness rather than just picking whatever jumps into their minds' eye. Meanwhile, their partners in Group B also begin C&E. If they are successful, their kundalini energy should energize their pineal glands—their psychic perception organs—and they should then be able to receive and reproduce the images their partners in Group A are sending to them. Afterward the roles are reversed and Group B will send to Group A.

Ramtha may set some limits. For example, he will suggest that the subject be a scene familiar to the sender, or an animal, or, more limited still, a color. He will then vary the target and ask everyone to describe an object in a box that is not in the room. Even more ambitious, he will have students focus upon something that does not exist—a set of objects that must be assembled. For example, in one session in which I participated, the object turned out to be a model house, red with two floors. An object was on both floors. The house was assembled several days after the students tried to perceive it.

For thirty years I have sat in on many groups that use a similar technique. Some degree of ESP seems to be a natural human ability, just as is playing a musical instrument or solving a calculus problem. If you pay attention to it, you get better at it, you learn what changes in consciousness and body feelings attend success, and you come to know what you can perceive and what you cannot. If you socialize with people to whom ESP is an important aspect of life, and as you begin to share that opinion, you will begin to recognize psychic incidents occurring daily that you normally explain in more mundane terms (a hunch, a coincidence). (However, many conservative Christians attribute such occurrences to the actions of supernatural beings such as angels or demons.)

Repeating the sending-and-receiving exercise in a group helps students perfect their skills. Some students are quickly successful, and success is rewarded with the group's praise. Copies of matching pictures are posted for all to see. Early successes testify that it can be done and builds confidence as students see others do it. Increasing success comes with each new exercise, and over time students' skills are sharpened. Meanwhile, Ramtha praises those who succeed, but he does not condemn those who are slower. He encourages them and shows them how close to success they may be. He jokes with those who had received their partners' images but then, not trusting, drew something else. Eventually, they will learn to trust their perceptions.

103

Although students are focused on sending and receiving, they spend considerable time practicing C&E and finish the exercise being much more comfortable with focusing on images. And well they should be, for next they will be taken to the transformed horse-exercise track for the single most important and time-consuming practice: fieldwork, in more than one sense of the word.

ANALOGICAL MIND

Before turning to fieldwork, however, we need further insight into Ramtha's presentation of the subtle human anatomy, specifically the idea of *analogical mind*. Ramtha proposed the existence of a radiant field surrounding every object that takes on gross material existence, including the human body. Some people can see part of that field— termed the *aura*—and it can be photographed as a Kirlian field. Metaphysicians have generally thought of the aura as an energy field radiating outward from the body. Like the sun, its corona could flare out in some places (such as over a chakra) or in other places almost disappear altogether. Some psychics have spoken of a broken aura, the breaks being signs of ill health or personality disorders. Others reported seeing black splotches. Parapsychological testing has demonstrated that psychics' descriptions of auras are very subjective, based upon their understanding of auras and the significance of colors rather than upon objective perception.

In the 1970s Kirlian photographs revealed great irregularities in the energy field, originally thought to be indicative of changes in bodily or mental states. Researchers hoped the photographs would finally provide a means both of establishing this bit of psychic lore in the scientific world and of providing a way to discern bodily conditions. For several years having one's fingertips or hand photographed with a portable Kirlian device was the fad in psychic circles. However, the interesting effects that frequently appeared on those photographs are now known to have been entirely produced by inadequate controls when regulating the pressure between the body (usually a fingertip) and the photographic plate.[4]

Ramtha suggests that psychics misunderstood the nature of the body's energy field and in effect sent researchers on a wild goose chase. The energy field is not radiating from the body and giving off energy so much as it is produced by energy slowing and collapsing into gross matter. The energy that creates the aura carries the pattern of thought, which ultimately shapes the body and allows it to hold its form and structure. So, the auric field is not the product of the body. Quite the opposite: the body is the end result of the action of the energy field. As such it is fairly evenly present around the body at all times, though it may lose some of its brilliance as death approaches.

The energy field around the body, which begins a few inches from the body and extends outward several feet, is a rainbow of seven bands comprising a seven-level spectrum of energy frequencies. These frequencies also reflect the seven-level universal structure. Closest to the body is a rusty red-colored band of very slow energy radiating in the hertizan range.[5] In successive layers the bands are in the infrared, visible light, ultraviolet, X ray, and gamma ray frequencies. The seventh band's frequency is even higher and is termed the infinite unknown. The bands are normally pictured in a two-dimensional cross section around a frontal outline of the body, but the bands encase the three-dimensional body completely. They are in constant movement circulating around the body in a current.

Ramtha says there are two sets of bands. One set exists close into the body, its inner layers following the body contours rather closely. Beginning farther out beyond arm's length is a second set of layers with the same energy spectrum as that of the inner bands. It also swirls around the body. We perceive the world through both these energy bands.

Under normal consciousness we perceive the world with *binary* thinking (see figure 4). We think as separate beings who exist in a world with a multitude of separate objects. That perception is not wrong, and it has its necessary and proper function. However, it is also the perception in which limitations and boundaries operate, and if it is the only world in which we operate, such limitations and boundaries become straightjackets and prison bars to our thinking.

There is a second manner of perceiving in which we become one with the object of our perception. That form of perception is termed *analogical* thinking (see figure 5). At times, when consciousness is altered, when the majority of electromagnetic impulses produced by the brain are in the alpha frequency range, we momentarily perceive the world analogically. For example, our dreams are often so lifelike that we can easily mistake them for our waking world. For those moments we become one with the objects

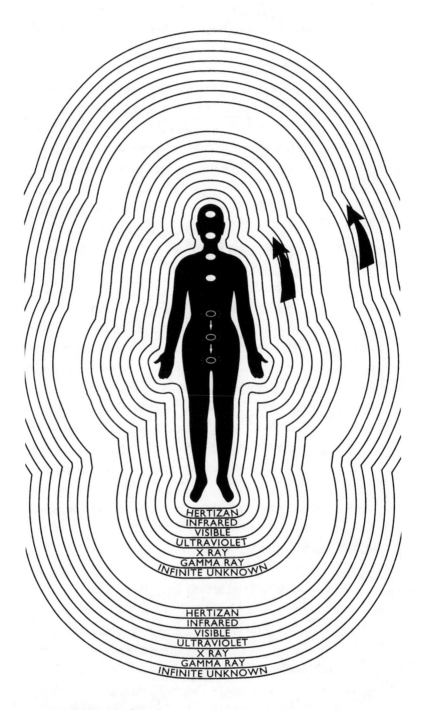

Figure 4. Binary Thinking

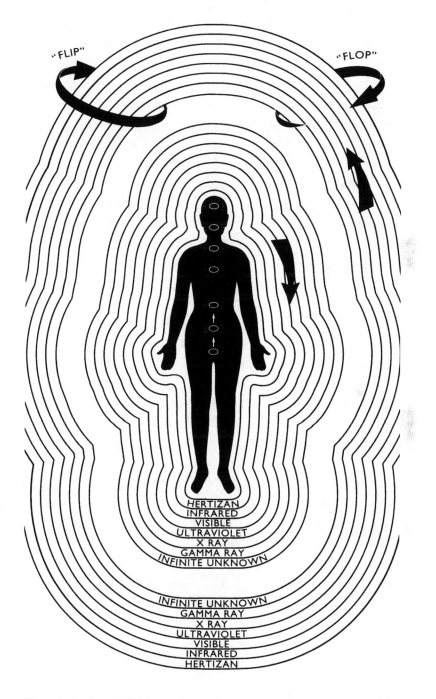

Figure 5. Analogical Thinking

of our perception—we perceive analogically. We also perceive analogically when we have sudden flashes of psychic awareness or knowingness. And when we are thinking analogically, according to Ramtha, a change occurs in the bands. The outer band flips over, the inner band changes direction, and both bands begin to circulate in opposite directions, creating an electromagnetic field. They become the energy correlates of the new form of envisioning the world. The most common time we are in alpha frequency is as we go into or come out of sleep. Therefore, one major goal of C&E practice is to produce analogical perception and to create the ability to exist in that state for extended periods without falling asleep. With that understanding and language, we can plunge ahead into the next exercise.

FIELDWORK

Originally I had been pushed into the middle of fieldwork like a kid thrown into a pool and told to sink or swim. Later, I was given a proper introduction with a group of beginning students. To begin the exercise, Ramtha instructed each of us to take two index-type cards and draw on each a symbolic picture of a wish or a desire. At the time I was completing a writing project, and on one of my cards I drew a mountain peak with a book possessing wings, the idea being the successful completion of the writing assignment on schedule, every writer's goal. The cards were then collected. Later, blindfolds in hand, we marched to the field and saw our cards taped face down on the fence. We got the idea that somehow our task would be to find at least one of them.

Before we began, Ramtha explained the rules. We were to sit, begin with C&E, and focus on the image of one of our cards. Then, when we felt ready we were to get up, spin around several times, and, keeping our focus on one of our cards and breathing periodically to energize the image, walk to where it was taped on the fence. Whenever we arrived at the fence, we were allowed to lift the blindfold and look at the card directly in front of us. If it was ours, we shouted our discovery. If it was not, we were to quickly replace the card and blindfold, turn from the fence, refocus on our card, and move into the field again.

Then Ramtha talked briefly about some problems that would arise. First, some would feel a great need to succeed, and indeed, those who succeeded would be warmly praised at the end of the day. After a while, if we did not find our card, we may be tempted to cheat. When we reached the fence, for example, we might look at several nearby cards. After all, everyone was blindfolded, so who would know? Or, we might walk in small circles near the fence so that we could quickly return to it a few feet from our latest position.

As with any endeavor, of course, cheating missed the point. At the school it would lead students to a dead end. Also, Ramtha, who regularly stayed in the field as gamemaster, did not take kindly to people wasting their tuition fees in this manner and said that anyone caught cheating would have to sit in the school's equivalent of the corner—outside the fence. (The only occasion I can remember seeing Ramtha approach a temperament I might call anger was during a discussion of this issue, and cheating on fieldwork is the only occasion I know of for which anyone was singled out for failure to perform.)

Previously, I had been led into the field, given a blindfold, and invited to participate. I had little idea of what was occurring. It must be a simple exercise in clairvoyance, I had surmised, and the idea was to locate the card, as in remote viewing, and go to it. I was to see the location in my mind's eye and find my way there. The blindfold was merely an additional obstacle that in its own way helped (by blocking interfering light stimuli) because it provided an interesting twist and hindrance. Having not yet grasped the essence of C&E or analogical thinking, however, I had been playing a game different from what the students had been playing. The difference was the distinction between passive reception of neutral information (that is, clairvoyance, still in a binary mode) and active creation of reality by energizing a willed thought (and analogically becoming one with it). Fieldwork amounts to entering into and

109

holding a hypnogogic state while walking around the field, thereby entering the vision created in the mind's eye to the extent that one forgets its relative unreality from a binary perceptive mode.

In short, students create symbolic reality on their cards and reproduce that reality by consciously focusing on them in their minds' eye. When the existence of what was willed and symbolized is accepted, it becomes one with the new reality. That reality now exists, and it is only a matter of time before it is visible to everyone. This is the essence of the creative process; hence, the new reality should manifest initially by students finding their cards on the fence, a culminating part of the game. (Of course, finding one card does not end the game; it continues to the second card.)

Fieldwork is thus the great reality-shaping game. It is non-competitive, ultimately, after students understand it. In the beginning each person who finds a card means that others can, too. And each person who does not find a card helps others not feel so bad after all. Every student wins, the prize being whatever was on the card. What another student did or did not do is irrelevant—in the long run.

The field is also a psychological pressure cooker. Students learn to hold their focus for a few seconds, then for a few minutes, and then for extended periods. In between those periods of focus, all their psychological garbage and conflicting training instructions surface. Students must learn to hold focus in spite of sound distractions, other people moving around them, the irregular surface upon which they walk, and bodily functions that demand attention (such as pressure on their bladders or aches in their legs). Like good marines, if they are to get through Ramtha's boot camp, they must learn that they cannot allow themselves to be ruled by their bodies' demands.

After several sessions, students have extended their comfort zones and the fun of the first half-hour of fieldwork now extends to several hours or—perish the thought—half a day or longer. Then conditions begin to vary. The field is in Washington, a state with four seasons. I have (from a distance) watched students doing fieldwork in pouring rain and on ground freshly covered with snow. (Students quickly learn that boots, long underwear, jeans, and full-length ponchos are part of an aspiring master's necessary and fashionable apparel.)

Between events at the school, all the feelings that arose during fieldwork—phobias, irrational hatred of Ramtha and its acting-out toward others, a sense of inadequacy, questions of why one is wasting valuable time engaged in this silly game—are considered and worked on. Many students reported that their most vivid memories of fieldwork, especially early on, were the personal issues it forced upon them and the changes it demanded in light of Ramtha's teachings. As issues arose, they had to juxtapose those issues beside his teachings and their past actions, and then choose between the two. Many have chosen to leave, most during the first year, some after working in the advanced group for several years. Some reported going so far with the work and then dropping out for several years, returning only when they felt ready.

One's career in the school is, however, tied to fieldwork. It is the most constant factor in a curriculum that is undergoing constant change as the advanced class progresses and as Ramtha finds better ways of presenting his teachings. The most advanced students still do fieldwork. As such, the cards made for fieldwork become an important part of the new culture the students are creating. During events, cards students find while doing fieldwork are taped to the fronts of their shirts and proudly displayed. At the end of each day, Ramtha calls upon all who have found their cards to rise and receive not only his acknowledgment but that of the student body. On one occasion JZ invited me to see the wall where her cards were displayed. As JZ, she, too, is Ramtha's student and is quite proud of her accomplishments in fieldwork, limited to those rare occasions when Ramtha leaves the students to continue on their own.

Although fieldwork is almost a constant in the students' lives, there are other disciplines. One particularly raises the pressure felt in the field—the tank.

111

THE TANK

Shortly after the school was founded, Ramtha instructed that a large labyrinth be built. Its outside wall forms a circle some 120 feet in diameter. The inside walls are completely mobile so the pattern of the labyrinth is often altered. The entrance also can be moved. All the walls are high (eight feet) and are strong enough so that several staff members can walk on top while a new pattern is being created or be present during an exercise in case a problem develops. The first tank experiences occurred in March 1990 at an advanced student retreat.

The object of the tank game is simple: find the center, termed the Void. Students focus not on self-generated images so much as what has previously been described as Point Zero. Although Ramtha's philosophy pictures Point Zero as located upward through the levels, psychologically it lies within, in the center of one's self, symbolized by the center of the labyrinth.

112

Students encounter several obstacles (it would not be much of a game without them). For example, at one point they must get on their hands and knees to fit through a low passageway. There is also a bridgelike ramp over which they must pass. At several points, they may encounter ladders over a wall. After climbing the wrong ladder, they can even find themselves outside the tank, in which case they have to go back to the entrance and start over.

The tank, like the field, also presents auxiliary problems. For example, students enter the tank en masse. So many people taking up limited space quickly affects anyone with even the smallest bit of claustrophobia. And if claustrophobia or the frustration of being trapped by a group of bodies blocking a passageway weren't enough, Ramtha has introduced additional rules. Initially, students were led to the front door and as they entered put on their blindfolds. Now they usually put them on before leaving the assembly hall and must find their way to the tank entrance some two hundred yards away through the school's parking lot. If they miss the entrance, there is no need to fear; the wooded area beyond the tank is ready to receive them, and they can entertain themselves walking in it for a portion of the day! However, after a brief period of wandering, beginning students are assisted back to the entrance.

I have yet to experience the tank, but one of Ramtha's more well-known and outspoken students, actress Linda Evans, was willing to share her experience. Evans, who came to the school as a fairly accomplished practitioner in the New Age world, had one of her most profound personal growth experiences while using the tank. As a newly advanced student, she missed the entrance and wound up in the woods. Getting lost was not the problem, and the mud—who cares? But in the woods she encountered not only trees but also large bushes with sharp, needlelike thorns. Evans is not just an actress but a well-paid beautiful leading lady. In the woods she faced the threat of physical damage that could directly harm her professional image. She had to choose which values would control her actions. After several moments of self-examination she made her choice, took her hands from her face, and finally made her way to the tank entrance.

113

Ramtha has also stretched the time for using the tank, sometimes to most of a day. Rumors of the pressures students experienced became an item of gossip in Yelm, and questions were raised during one of the court cases involving the school. One local newspaper, in a story raising questions about the "mysterious" practices at the school, sent a plane over the school grounds to photograph the labyrinth, which dominated the next day's front page.

OTHER PRACTICES

Ramtha's school can be thought of as a spiritual survival camp. Details of the practices, following time-honored esoteric tradition, are revealed to students step-by-step. It is an intense training that not only presents a new worldview but provides initiatory practices to speed up the attainment of what most metaphysical systems suggest will take a lifetime, if not multiple lifetimes. The teachings also form a connected whole structure; that is, any part of the teachings separated from the whole can appear at times incomprehensible, offensive, subversive, overly demanding, or just plain silly. However, in the context of the training, the practices Ramtha provides embody the teachings as they unfold. Most practices illustrate an immediate teaching, although they also provide a cumulative secondary effect of improving old skills. A few practices allow students to comprehend a teaching they may not have understood during a previous practice. Several practices also come as pleasant relief following an intense period of sitting in lecture sessions or doing fieldwork. For example, the free-form "pagan dancing" accompanied by loud music breaks up the heaviness and intensity of some exercises.

Additional practices vary widely. One, called *tahumo*, challenges students to test their ability to withstand cold weather by creating internal body heat.[6] More tame is the practice, now adopted by most advanced students, of creating a list of goals around which daily C&E focus is concentrated. As items on the list manifest, they are removed and new items added. Such lists are quite diverse but will usually include items for personal improvement, material items, health goals, and attaining the next level of teachings.

One set of practices, built around the concept of the fourth level and the blue body, deserves special notice because of both its importance to the advanced students and its uniqueness in the larger esoteric world.

THE BLUE BODY

One aspect of Gnosticism that makes it so attractive is its visual nature—it can be drawn on the blackboard and introduced in pictures. The universe is a stairway with seven steps, a ladder with seven rungs; the metaphors can be multiplied indefinitely. Different worlds can be imagined by calling up the images associated with each level of reality. However, one major step in understanding the Gnostic system is by putting aside the spatial metaphors and grasping the cosmology as a symbolic code aimed at communicating a new psychology of the self. Thus, in Ramtha's terms Point Zero is not at the other end of the universe but is a focal point in the depth of consciousness. The astral body does not exist in some astral realm or the light body in some light realm; they both reside in the same space as does the physical body.[7] Ultimately, making this jump in perception is essential to Ramtha's presentation of the blue body.

To Ramtha, a definitive break is made between the third (light) and fourth (ultraviolet) levels of existence. Remember that during creation the move from the fourth to the third level is the occasion of the big bang. When the gods wished to make significant changes in the structure of the physical body by adding sex organs, they worked from the fourth level. After death, the move beyond the third-level light body is a difficult but necessary step to make if meaningful individual evolution is to happen. Both the third-level light body and the second-level astral body reflect the imperfections of the physical body. Thus, free access to the fourth-level ultraviolet realm beyond the third-level light realm is a necessary step for meaningful change.

One set of teachings for advanced students is training to access the fourth level. The perfect symbol of this work is the ancient Hindu deity Shiva, and as a visible sign that Ramtha was about to introduce the blue body teachings, several years ago a huge painting of Shiva was placed on the wall of the main assembly hall.

From a distance, the painting appears like traditional pictures of Shiva as a physical body painted blue. In fact, Ramtha teaches that it is a body of energy vibrating in the ultraviolet range and thus appears blue. It is not solid so much as it is a body consisting of numerous lines of swirling energy that have coalesced into a shape resembling the human body, but with some very important differences. It is genderless. Shiva, that is, the blue body, possesses no penis, womb, or mammary glands. It also lacks any imperfections of the physical body because it has no particularities of the individual body. It houses all the potential of human existence, including the potential for healing, says Ramtha.

The blue body can be accessed through disciplines taught by Ramtha. From the beginning of Ramtha's introduction of the blue body teachings and continuing as students work with the techniques, many healings have been reported. To some extent, the presence of such healings, common to many groups that do spiritual healing, is not a sign of the truth of the teachings, though the absence of them would be significant. However, some of the school's reported healings have been noteworthy and a few spectacular. They include everything from the healing of a wasp sting in a person with a history of allergic reactions to a man who had been diagnosed with terminal prostate cancer. By far the most extraordinary healing was the regrowth of lost permanent teeth.[8]

SPIRITUAL FORMATION?

Taken as a set, the practices offered are analogous to the system of spiritual formation that may be taught to future priests in a Roman Catholic seminary or pursued over the years with the assistance of a spiritual director. Each uses different approaches to a spiritual world, but in the long run broad areas of agreement would begin to manifest because the object of both is the exploration of the inner consciousness. We all have an inner world of conscious memories, thoughts, beliefs, and vivid dreams. However, our interesting personal quest begins as that world is left behind and the far countries that lie inside, beyond those boundaries, are explored. Numerous are the techniques to explore and the metaphors to describe that region. They vary from traditional religious and mystical metaphors to magic, Freudian or Jungian psychotherapy, or Gnosticism. Some of us will explore timidly and some with great boldness. Most of us will find hostile neighbors who must by some means be pacified. But we all are entering the same land, though it will look very different according to the knowledge and ideas we bring to our quest.

It would be superficial to think of the students as blindly following a very talented teacher. It would be simply false to reduce our appraisal of what they are attempting to the effects of brainwashing. However much I may disagree with Ramtha's ideas, I have no doubt that his students are engaged in long-term serious quests, however unusual, for the meaning of life. In Ramtha's philosophy they have found a sophisticated theological world capable of engaging their intellect, and in the practices they have discovered a workable system that facilitates their coming to grips with the intellectual content.

That being the case, seeing Ramtha's teachings as a bold (he would, I am sure, prefer *outrageous*) system of spiritual formation is the best way to bring together this seemingly odd collection of "unspiritual" practices so integral to the curriculum. Somewhere along their process of growth, students begin to demonstrate the recognizable passion so integral to the mystical literature, and when that passion arises, their value systems relative to the larger social world shift dramatically, in the same way they do in all deeply committed religious souls. Out of their feeling of attunement to the larger metaphysical world, they develop a sense of oneness with all life and creation. They become concerned for the welfare of their neighbors, they reorient life on the higher values (truth, beauty, goodness), and they develop a thirst for spiritual reality. Although one would not predict the emergence of anything like a Christian mystical piety, one can expect to see something like traditional mysticism—but appropriate to Ramtha's teachings—appear. But the school is just beginning, and I am not a prophet. Like everyone else, I shall just have to wait and see.

117

7

LIFE AT
RAMTHA'S
SCHOOL TODAY

The school has evolved at a rapid pace, the changes being driven both by the growing size of the student body and by the need to accommodate the increasing gap between beginning and advanced students. By 1995, Ramtha had established a standard curriculum of both mandatory and optional classes for new students. All new students attend a two-day Level 1 Beginning C&E Workshop. Next, new students attend a one-week Level 2 Beginning C&E Retreat. Finally, they attend the three-day Level 3 Beginning C&E Follow-up, which prepares them to be integrated into the current student body. At least once a year Levels 1 and 2 events are held close together to accommodate students, both foreign and domestic, who travel long distances to attend. Students who have finished all their levels are then integrated into the advanced groups.

During the three levels, Ramtha introduces students to all the currently active spiritual disciplines (since 1988 some practices have been replaced with others of a similar nature) so they will be prepared to join students in the disciplines of the two mandatory advanced events: a seven-day retreat in the spring and a three-day follow-up in the fall. Students who miss the mandatory events must repeat the initial beginning levels before they can be reintegrated into the advanced group.

At times, Ramtha has rewarded the efforts of a class by granting a special privilege (such as dropping tuition for some events, inviting class members to an advanced event, or holding a special event just for that class). As each class progresses through its work, it is given a name. To date six names have been assigned. The first group in 1988 was named Elohim. Subsequent groups were named in 1989 (Akh Men Ra); 1990 (Europa Akh Men Ra, Om Akad); 1991, 1992, and 1993 (Iaut Aleph); 1994, 1995, and 1996 (Iaut Aleph/Sun and Moon); and May 1996 (Elohim Ka Men Ra). At one point, these names roughly designated levels of attainment in the school, but over the last few years such distinctions have been blurred and now primarily tell fellow students which class someone went through.

Students may attend optional events, such as Assays. Assays provide lengthy periods—a week to ten days—for intensive discipline practice of mind over matter and space. In addition, the school holds advanced group events, some on practice and some with lectures either by Ramtha or by specially invited guests. Parties (with a purpose) are held at Halloween and over the winter holidays. Of all the special events, among the most well attended is Boktau, a month-long retreat held in summer.

THE RAMTHA CULTURE

One standard by which religious communities are evaluated is their production of culture. And all successful new religions express their lives in high-quality artistic works. Even Ramtha's School of Enlightenment, though still relatively small and only a decade old, has already inspired an artistic life within the community.

During one event I noticed that along with the more familiar music being played was one piece I had never heard before, and in spite of my love for bluegrass, it impressed me. It was a high-energy piece with a good beat but without the "noise" I associate with most rock music. I was sitting next to Debbie Christie, the young woman controlling audio, and was thus able to ask her about the piece. She said that she was the artist, and eventually she shared a tape with me, because the work was not yet published. Debbie, it seems, had joined the staff as a volunteer in 1988 and began to select and mix the music used at events. Eventually, she was hired to handle the sound chores for all events. She said that throughout her life she was inhibited by her bad self-image. She played in the band in high school and college but did not become a music major (what she really wanted) because of fear of playing solo in front of an audience. Then, she held back on her composing because she thought she lacked the training or ability to do it the way she wished. The turning point was a brief give-and-take with Ramtha one day soon after joining the staff. He complemented her on her choice of music for an event. She blurted out, "But I just wish it was my own." He looked directly at her and replied, "One day you will be playing your own music in the arena." It was not until 1993, however, that she risked using her creative abilities. With several friends she composed a piece called "Snake Charmer." She described her reaction: "Boy, was I jazzed." Other pieces followed, including one with Diane O'Keefe, another student. Then, in 1994 she published "Dancing Drums" (the piece that I had fallen in love with) and the equally enjoyable "Shiva." Although I initially thought both "Dancing Drums" and "Shiva" were just beautiful pieces of music, I later understood how the music had flowed out of the integration of her music and her experiences as a student.

121

Debbie's music called my attention to the group's other artistic expressions, which I soon noticed in the school's bookstore: several periodicals with names like *Awakenings*, *Focus*, and *The Golden Thread*. I began picking up the latest issues each time I visited the ranch. In their pages I discovered a lively literary culture inspired by Ramtha's teachings. Issues of *Awakenings*, for example, include essays from a variety of contributors, short autobiographical stories, and reflections on contemporary events. *Focus* specializes in additional comment on science and related topics Ramtha has discussed as well as interviews and articles by experts whose books Ramtha recommends. *The Golden Thread* seems dedicated to exploring the practical consequences of Ramtha's teachings (such as how one implements a self-sufficient lifestyle) and to exploring ideas currently of interest within the student body.[1]

I soon discovered that Christie and the drumming group she organized were but a small part of the musical arts at the school. Other composer-musicians—Carl Schafner, Nick Humphreys, and Scott Ercoloni—are beginning to make their presences felt. Soon, perhaps, a significant amount of music heard at the school may be students' products. And the artistic life has not been confined to the school. Danielle Brosco, another student, has organized a dance company composed mostly of students. It performs throughout the Pacific Northwest and Canada.

Art is beginning to make a visual impact as students transform Ramtha's verbal images into paintings. The hall is now dominated by two reproductions: *Shiva* and Michelangelo's *Creation of Adam*, executed by long-term students Don Marshall and Gary Craig. In the fall of 1994, an original painting called *Cosmic Being* was reproduced on both large posters and sweatshirts. The value of such skill was recognized, and a committee was formed to encourage and facilitate artistic expression.

RAMTHA'S STUDENTS

After I attended several school events, especially the beginning one, I realized that Ramtha was not attracting what is usually thought of as the standard recruit to a new religion. The people who gathered appeared to be much older, more mature. That impression was reinforced when I began to quantify the questionnaires students had so graciously filled out for me. The school was six years old. The average age for advanced students was early forties and for beginning students, thirties. I was wondering about both groups being older than common wisdom would have supposed until I remembered what my psychotherapist friend

Robert L. Moore had taught me many years ago when we worked together on a textbook on the new religions.

Moore had pointed out that there are specific periods in our lives (as average Westerners) when we are in transition and are relatively free to make choices about changing significant aspects of our lives.[2] In such times we enter a state in which we question our previous values and the basic structures that underpin our lives. This usually occurs in late adolescence as we make the move to adulthood, and we make some long-term choices about such matters as jobs and careers and sexual self-images. We are also expected to make mature decisions about religious commitments. Because most of us make the transition from adolescence to adulthood at approximately the same time, those who change religions (not just move from one church to another similar church) will do so between the ages of eighteen and twenty-five. New religions quickly learn this fact and concentrate their efforts on recruiting young adults. But Ramtha's school does not engage in much recruiting activity (prospective students must contact the school first), and it definitely does not make special efforts to reach young adults.

However, Moore also pointed out that there is a secondary, albeit important, transition stage generally known as the midlife crisis. This term covers a much broader range of phenomena and generally occurs between thirty-five and forty-five years of age. Ramtha has had significant appeal to people who have already experienced life and have gained some degree of maturity but who have reached unsatisfying places in their lives. He speaks particularly to women who are in the process of discovering their power and appreciate his choice of JZ through whom to speak.[3] Mary Redhead, an original student of Ramtha's teachings, is one of those women.

Redhead had many years of experience as an entrepreneur in the metaphysical world. She saw in Ramtha something extraordinary, and as Ramtha's movement grew, his followers also became her main customers.

123

In the beginning, Ramtha had been for Redhead but a small step to a slightly better metaphysical teacher. Little had really changed in her life; she had simply shifted her need to be dependent onto Ramtha. Like so many, even to some extent JZ herself, Redhead had not caught on to Ramtha's general disdain for anything approaching guru worship. She still had a few doubts about Ramtha's genuineness; she wanted to accept and staunchly affirm the truth of his message of self-divinity and the great potential anyone could manifest.

Redhead became the senior person on JZ's staff, the one who fielded questions both from JZ and her less experienced helpers and from the public eager to know more. Then, around 1982 at one of the dialogues, Ramtha walked up to her and, without any hint of what he was about to do, in his commanding voice said, "Leave my audience and don't come back!" Redhead was at the moment dealing with her doubts; Ramtha had now hurt and publicly humiliated her. When JZ was told what had transpired, she fired Redhead. Redhead's social and business world crumbled, precipitating her midlife crisis.

The separation became a time for severe self-examination. Redhead eventually gained new insight about her self-doubts and saw that although she articulated metaphysical truths quite well, she did not really embody them. With this new understanding, she reinterpreted Ramtha's actions as a great kindness to her.

A year or two later Redhead had worked through her crisis, had reestablished herself as an independent businesswoman, and had overcome her self-doubts. She knew it was time to go back, and quietly she slipped into the audience during a dialogue. Ramtha immediately interrupted what he was doing, walked to her, placed his hand on her, and simply called her name. She knew that she had completed her transition. Like the prodigal returned, she was immediately accepted back into the fold, no questions asked.

The next part of Redhead's story has become part of the school's folklore. After her return, Redhead was at one of the desert retreats Ramtha held in the mid-1980s. Ramtha walked around the assembly as he was prone to do and approached her. As he came closer, her body began to shake so that she felt she was going to fall off the chair. She suddenly looked in Ramtha's direction, and instead of seeing JZ she saw Ramtha, all seven-plus feet of him. They carried on a brief conversation. When she returned to normal consciousness, she could not remember the content of the conversation, though all the audience heard it. And, for some reason, it was not on the tape of the session. She later understood that Ramtha had raised the frequency of her body (hence the sensations of shaking) in such a way that she could see him. She now interprets the event as a gift to her, an acknowledgment of her growth and her understanding of his prior actions.

In the numerous stories Ramtha's students shared with me, I heard many similarities. Many with college and even postgraduate training reported giving up their careers to work at semiskilled or unskilled jobs in search of a happier way of being in the world. They overwhelmingly tell either of Ramtha as the culmination of a long search for meaning and purpose or of a voice interrupting a frustrating life situation by offering a new direction.

Many women redirected their energies from their families, who no longer needed the bulk of their time. One woman in her fifties announced to her family that in the next decade she would be redirecting her life to handling the lack she felt in herself. At the time she had no particular direction, but the following February she attended a beginning event at the ranch. As she put it, "I knew I had found what I was looking for." It took her a year to rearrange her life so she could go through the entire curriculum, but in 1991 she joined the student body permanently. She reflected on the intervening years: "The fact that God is *not* 'out there' but here inside of me, I think, was the most startling revelation, and that I am capable of doing everything that Jeshua ben Joseph has done and so can everyone."

Another woman, who had been divorced, told of beginning a spiritual search that led originally to an evangelical Christian

125

congregation in her native land. However, she found it unsatisfying, though she is thankful for its introducing her to the teachings of Jesus. A friend had attended a beginner's weekend, so the woman started reading some Ramtha books and listening to his tapes. Finally, in 1992 she attended her first event and has been a student ever since. She says, "Ramtha's teachings bring out, through experience, the inner self and my powers of the mind in such a way that make me know I am more than my human self. And the changes I unfold are real and permanent—I don't just make a role—I become my real self."

One man in his fifties, a divorced engineer, first encountered Ramtha in 1988. On a video he heard Ramtha's question, "Who owns you?" as an inquiry directly to him. He was already searching through other spiritual groups, but soon he sold his business and moved to British Columbia. He now is a semiretired farmer and Ramtha student.

One forty-four-year-old married chemical engineer from Houston spoke of devoting fifteen years primarily to her family, during which time she discovered Ramtha's videos. In 1986 she and her husband attended a dialogue in Atlanta. For her the message that there was no need to experience death, that life goes on, was crucial. Ramtha was the first to confirm what she had felt since childhood: that death did not have to be the end of one's life. Several years ago she and her husband moved to Washington and started an engineering company.

Recently, sociologist Constance Jones completed a study of advanced students, from which we can construct a profile.[4] A majority of respondents were female. They are well educated with almost 40 percent having finished college. They tend to be employed in high-prestige positions in the professions, technology, or business. Many are self-employed. Typically, they are in midlife, have achieved high levels of education and occupational prestige, and are now choosing to orient themselves in a new direction.

Jones's work also confirmed my conclusions, partially from the array of books in the bookstore, that the student body includes many intelligent, independent, well-read people. More than 40 percent came to Ramtha after exposure to the New Age movement, and more than 50 percent had read the White Book prior to attending an event. Feeling disconnected from their earlier, more conventional lives, they have accepted the wisdom of a nonconventional spiritual teacher, often at some personal sacrifice. And they have found a community in which subjects discounted by the mainstream culture can be explored. Thus, it is not surprising that several ideas Ramtha discusses, even though they are not central to the primary teachings on enlightenment, have found some acceptance among the students.

EARTH CHANGES

Early in the dialogues, Ramtha began to speak to a range of topics of special interest to students who were part of the larger New Age culture. Brief discussions on such topics as soul mates and Earth changes led to weekend intensives devoted to one topic. Although these topics fall outside the main curriculum, and many students pay little attention to them, other students find them fascinating and will have no difficulty striking up a conversation on UFOs, artificial structures on the moon, crop circles, or holistic health remedies.[5] Two such topics have had a measurable effect upon the student body: Ramtha's teachings on Earth changes added incentive for some students to move to Washington near the school, and some students found in the teachings on the Graymen an element at odds with what they had considered Ramtha's earlier, positive messages.

Ramtha's teachings on Earth changes cannot be understood apart from ideas prevalent within the New Age movement. For example, seer Edgar Cayce's channeled material, made popular in the 1960s, prophesied several significant Earth changes occurring during the last quarter of the twentieth century. In readings scattered throughout the decades between the two world wars, Cayce predicted among other things that in about 1968 a portion of

127

Atlantis would rise again, that in the 1940s new land would appear in both the Atlantic and Pacific oceans, and that by the end of the century not only would portions of Georgia and the Carolinas disappear, but so would New York City.

These and other predictions were compiled by Jeffrey Goodman in his 1978 book, *We Are the Earthquake Generation.* Psychics he quoted had concluded that by 1990 most of the western United States would disappear; the land separating the Great Lakes would sink, turning the lakes into one vast midcontinental lake; and Earth's axis would tip by several degrees. These prophecies were associated with the most famous prediction, now almost a classic bit of American folklore, of California's fall into the sea because of action along the San Andreas Fault.[6]

Ramtha was identified with these doomsday prophets, not altogether without reason, although he clearly separated himself from them. The prophecies of disaster prompted Merv Griffin's question during Ramtha's 1985 television appearance: "Are we in danger on this planet of any major catastrophe?" Ramtha answered those who were predicting significant Earth changes and a possible war with China or the Soviet Union:

> It shan't ever be war that will destroy. That is not the great holocaust, entity. It is nature . . . diseasements. Indeed. That is already here, and yet it will grow even more vast. It is greater than any bomb that could have ever been dropped. Know you who created the disease? Mankind. For they have the power within them to do that—it is from their attitude. Now that is no holocaust. They have done these things and manifested these things for a learning—to gain wisdom . . . the appreciation of what they call their enemies. They will learn through this to love their enemies. That is a grand teaching. The earth will never be destroyed. It will not rotate on its axis. No one is going to drop bombs on it. It will go on and on. But the greater "consciousness" is coming.[7]

Ramtha did suggest that contemporary society would be shaken by great natural catastrophes, which would include a significant drought in the U.S. Midwest during 1987–1989 (which occurred). The pole would not change and World War III was not in the future. Changes were to be viewed not so much as troubles to be anticipated but as spurs to evolution. Disasters were coming, but they would occur over time and space and each one rather limited in its damage. For example, when in Sydney, Australia, for the first time, Ramtha predicted a tidal wave would hit the city but did not suggest the destruction of the city or major decimation of part of the subcontinent.

However, Ramtha did suggest that Washington was a relatively safe haven. Although the reaction to natural forces was always (and remains) a relatively minor theme in Ramtha's teachings, it spoke strongly to some New Age students. At least one weekend dialogue was devoted to exploring the issue, and Ramtha's comments were transcribed into a book.[8]

129

Ramtha's warning touched some people more deeply than others. It added strength and will to people already feeling trapped in unhappy situations, not a few facing their midlife crises, and occasioned their joining the migration to what many have seen as America's last frontier. For some, the move to Washington was coincidental with the breakup of a marriage, and angry spouses were quick to blame JZ, leader of the Ramtha "cult" perceived as the source of the breakup. In 1987–1988 the heated words of a few disgruntled spouses added fuel to the torch fires of the crowd that sought to destroy the monster who lived in the castle outside Yelm, by which time more than five hundred people had relocated. They added their strength to the many followers who already lived in the greater Seattle-Tacoma-Olympia urban area.[9]

For most who relocated, the move was part of a lifestyle transformation. It usually involved a change in occupation, either to escape the rat race or to explore undeveloped areas of their lives. Some gave up lucrative careers and took subsistence-level or part-time jobs that allowed them to attend events at the school and to pursue their schoolwork between events. The relative freedom granted by a divorce or other life-crisis event presented the opportunity to live a life about which they had only (secretly) fantasized.

Personal changes were also integrated into the goal of self-sufficiency Ramtha encouraged. Followers gathered food and supplies to last for two years in case a catastrophe, personal or natural, interrupted the flow of food and other necessities. A few developed a perspective bordering on survivalism.[10] Many students realized for the first time that they could survive and progress apart from familiar supportive structures, that they not only possessed potential they had never actualized but that they were completely unaware they had it.

The initial wave of people arrived in Washington in 1986, and through 1987 and 1988 family members left behind expressed anger and concern. By 1989 a few residents of Yelm, aware of unwanted changes in their town (including the sudden increase in real estate prices) they attributed to the influx of students, began to express their anger openly. Over time that anger has died as townspeople ascribed changes more to the growth of western urban centers than to Ramtha students and as town leaders began to appreciate the economic boom the school represented to the community.

During the five years I have observed the school, I have noticed the lessening of tension between residents and students. I also had the opportunity to see students react to several natural disasters including flooding and a record snowfall that took out electricity for a week. The teachings on self-sufficiency served them well. Not only were they able to take the extraordinary weather in stride, but also they were able to assist their less-prepared neighbors.[11]

THE GRAYMEN

In one of the last dialogues prior to founding the school, Ramtha returned to one of his favorite themes, victimization and sovereignty. In this case, however, he approached his topic through a consideration of the social order. Blocking one's path to *sovereign* self-sufficiency, he said, was control of the economic order by international bankers. He acknowledged his agreement with an older theory of global conspiracy that began in France during the Napoleonic Era. The first Grayman was the financier-banker who supplied Napoleon with the financial resources necessary for conquest. Mayer Anselm Rothschild (1743–1812) differed from other bankers of the era in that he realized that to be successful in financing war, he could not give allegiance to any nation. The Rothschilds financed both sides of a conflict and even generated new conflicts that they subsequently financed and from which they profited. Over the centuries, the Graymen included other families, and collectively they have influenced governments and planned wars. They took control of the media in order to manipulate public opinion, which typically resisted hostilities.

The Graymen also created paper money to replace gold, then created the equivalent of the Federal Reserve in each country to print money as it saw fit to take further control of the economy. Loaning their money generously, they now have most world governments in their debt. Their goal is a One World Order embodied not in a united world government but in a World Bank. The instrument of control will be not an army but a universal debit card, the ultimate credit card, accepted anywhere. It will replace money and will dehumanize individuals into numbers that will follow us all our lives. The freedom of privacy will disappear.[12]

Students reacted in several ways to these teachings. Some simply ignored them; although they grew out of the basic teachings, they were not essential to the basic thrust toward masterhood. Still others reacted negatively. Some former members have complained that these teachings were not an expansion of Ramtha's philosophy but a new and contradictory teaching. Losing faith in JZ, they suggested that Ramtha had deserted JZ only to be replaced by a darker entity. In their disappointment, a

131

few became vocal critics of the school and were the source of repeated complaints that in the late 1980s Ramtha's teaching had turned in a dangerous, paranoid direction. Their complaints were circulating in the San Francisco Bay area as early as 1986 and were related by Jon Klimo in his 1987 book on channeling.[13] I first heard them when I began research on the *New Age Encyclopedia*, and I discovered that as JZ withdrew from appearances around the country, New Agers speculated about the change. Encouraged by ex-members, they began to ask if Ramtha had changed and found reason to answer in the affirmative with the publication of Ramtha's talks in *Ramtha Intensive: Change, the Days to Come* and *Last Waltz of the Tyrants*.

Certainly, if one saw the school primarily through the lens of Ramtha's teachings on the Graymen, one might expect to find a paranoid separatist student body led by a teacher warning his audience about outsiders. And in 1992 a group of former students charged that the school was rooted in fear, secrecy, and a demand for obedience and that it had become divisive with people competing for JZ's attention rather than seeking a higher state of consciousness. These charges alerted me to a possible problem.[14] However, in my five years of observing Ramtha's students, I have found no such paranoia. Instead, I have found students who were open, friendly, and set in their spiritual paths. They seem to have found a third way to integrate Ramtha's more recent teachings— as an additional spur encouraging them to overcome their sense of victimization and to move toward sovereign self-sufficiency. First, wake up to the situation and choose to be sovereign, understanding that self-sufficiency will best be found in the countryside. Then, store food and hard money (gold and silver) to shield one from the coming economic fluctuations. Pay off debts and live debt-free. After becoming self-sufficient, assist others to do likewise. Rather than concentrate upon evil, prepare for the worst and then live relatively free of the fear and anxiety that haunts those who live as victims of the world. And free of anxiety, go on with the major job of reaching enlightenment.

ON TO ASCENSION

Ramtha teaches a cosmology that is radically distinct from that held by most Westerners. Those who come as students are seekers. They are on pilgrimages to seek out a satisfactory spiritual worldview and are open to trying something new. Most are willing to participate in the spiritual disciplines with the same feeling of experimentation that has led them to attempt meditation or yoga or the martial arts. At the same time, resistance is great because the teachings not only adjust or replace older religious beliefs but attack the dominant social construction of reality that is passed on in school systems, assumed by the media, and confirmed in mundane experience.

Further, it is the outrageous and audacious aspect of Ramtha that he is attempting to lead, not just a few talented elites, but a whole community of otherwise average people (few are self-selected mystics, and none are withdrawing from the larger community into a monastery or convent) into a totally alternative worldview. In doing so, he has the task of convincing students not only that the new worldview can handle all the significant data from which the dominant worldview has been constructed but that it can account for far more data and provide a means to mastering the environment far more effectively than what it is replacing.

Ramtha is just getting started, for as of this writing the school is less than a decade old. His teachings continue to evolve as he introduces more material, primarily scientific, in an attempt to account for more data that confirm students' present experience, urges them on to further spiritual practice, and supports the overall worldview. Additional data, for example, are currently being added about the working of the human body, especially the central nervous system, with special reference to the manner in which the body facilitates the student's transformation.

Ramtha's School of Enlightenment is a new community as religious communities go, but even so it must offer some reflection not only on the first two great religious questions—the

133

origin of humanity and the meaning of this life—but also on the third: What is our destiny; that is, Where are we going as a result of all this effort? Ramtha has given a consistent answer to that question, though he rarely dwells on it. In this regard he uses the term *ascension*, a term popularized through the modern esoteric tradition, which become prominent in the 1990s. The term has also assumed a variety of meanings from one teacher to another.[15] Ramtha explains ascension as follows.

Ramtha teaches that bodily existence has been accomplished by the coagulation of energy from higher levels, each level embodying a particular thought. We, as entities, are born and presently exist as inhabited bodies to operate on this plane of existence. Properly awakened and trained, however, we should be able to speed up at will the vibration of the coagulated energy that composes our material substance and move into the next, or even higher, vibratory level.

134

In order to ascend—that is, to move into the next vibratory level without experiencing death and thus be able to return without again arriving via the birth canal—one must, according to Ramtha, "be born through the birth process, wholly maintain the integrity of self, and activate the entirety of the organ called the brain. Once you have opened your brain capacity to full use, you can, at will, command the body to raise its vibratory frequency to the point where it goes out of the frequency level of matter and into the vibratory frequency of light."[16] Death is leaving this plane without the body, and ascension is leave-taking with the body so one can return again without being born. That is the ultimate ability of a master, beyond the manifestation of needed financial resources, beyond healing the body, beyond stopping or even reversing the aging process.

Ramtha offers his students the hope that death is neither the end of life nor the end of the entities they are. Death is the result, ultimately, of the overwhelming judgment we place upon ourselves that we must die. But that is not our destiny. We need not continually die and come back only to die and come back again.

The process of getting rid of the judgment that we as humans have placed upon ourselves and then learning to ascend, however, is no easy matter. It is not simply a matter of believing in ascension. It is a difficult task. But it is the career Ramtha's students have chosen.

135

8

ON GROWING
A RELIGION IN A
HOSTILE ENVIRONMENT

As Ramtha became a New Age star, someone suggested to people with ABC-TV's *20/20* news magazine that Ramtha would be an ideal subject for an exposé. Here was a story made for television. A poor girl realized the American dream, but the dream had become a nightmare. The attractive woman had become a cult leader. Anyone with an adding machine could see that large sums of money (to most people) were moving through the organization. Also, given the size of the response to her work, there were bound to be a few dissatisfied students and disgruntled former employees. And given the nature of the unconventional ideas floating around Ramtha, there was plenty to snicker about. The television audience could be made to feel morally and intellectually superior. And the people at *20/20* had an unspoken double motivation: hostess Barbara Walters's husband had been a student before he married her. The show aired January 22, 1987.

20/20 STARTS DIGGING

In the months prior to the show, the *20/20* staff began to explore and quickly found the necessary handful of cooperative detractors. Among them emerged a philosophy professor in Denver

University's Department of Humanities, Carl Raschke. Early in his scholarly career, Raschke had written *The Interruption of Eternity*, a most competent volume tracing the history of Gnostic thought in the West. He had been concerned with its rebirth among otherwise professional nineteenth-century philosophers, such as Henri Bergson, and its popular spread in Theosophy and related groups. However, by the mid-1980s he had dismissed his book as merely a youthful intellectual exercise and had become incensed by the so-called real evils of the new "cults," especially the New Age movement. The movement had enough within it to disturb many 1980s academics, but Raschke had a deeper concern. He had become convinced that the New Age was masking a massive Satanic conspiracy. Raschke's fear of Satanism became public in 1985 at a large anti–New Age conference held at Denver Conservative Baptist Seminary and culminated in his book, *Painted Black*.[1]

Raschke appears to have been the first to target JZ. In 1986, even though he had not studied the movement and had admitted to being "caught with my pants down by the [channeling] craze," he was willing to go on record that JZ was either "disturbed or self-deluded." Although he had no psychological training, *Omni* magazine tapped him as a spokesperson for the psychological establishment, and Raschke was ready to offer his pop-psychological observations. He suggested that "most channels, after considerable study in metaphysical speculation and meditation techniques, attain a heightened sensitivity to their own unconscious minds. This hard-won internal receptiveness, this new voice, may then simply be interpreted as the voice of a god or spirit or ancestor or alien being by those emotionally predisposed to do so."[2] Through 1987, Raschke would move from merely dismissing JZ to parroting rhetoric concerning brainwashing and mind control and finally emerging as a mouthpiece of the anti-cult movement. He singled out Ramtha as an unethical teacher who taught his followers that there was no difference between right and wrong. He was featured on a panel at the 1987 convention of the Cult Awareness Network along with former student Carole Bowen, who complained of her brainwashing experience.

The *20/20* spot, however, presented a broad attack, based on six essential accusations:

1. JZ was a fraud. Basic to this charge was the testimony of a former staff member who complained that he had become disillusioned when he saw JZ put on and take off the Ramtha persona and, out of sight of her admiring followers, appeared to be practicing the Ramtha gestures.

2. JZ had defrauded her followers financially. *20/20* charged that JZ, as her Ramtha persona, had told gullible followers to invest in an Arabian horse business. Believers, unquestioning in their devotion, immediately did.

3. JZ had falsified details of her life in her autobiography. For example, people who were supposedly present when she claimed she saw a flying saucer in high school failed to verify the incident.

4. JZ was getting rich from her confidence scheme. JZ was no longer a poverty-stricken young woman or even a middle-class housewife. She was a multimillionaire, a perfect example of a wealthy cult leader who had bilked her followers out of large sums of money, primarily by charging excessive sums for attendance at Ramtha's performances.

5. Ramtha was a cult leader. Using the negative image surrounding new religions which the network of anti-cult groups create, *20/20* added its insight that the students were merely sheeplike followers of silly ideas to which no rational, thinking people could adhere unless they had been caught at vulnerable moments and brainwashed by a superficially attractive but morally decadent and manipulative leader. A sure sign of their brainwashed condition

139

was that so many had left jobs and homes to move to the Northwest because they had believed some of Ramtha's apocalyptic assertions about coming Earth changes.

6. Ramtha was dangerously immoral in teaching believers that they were divine and hence lived beyond any moral imperative concerning right or wrong. If Ramtha's students lived beyond the law, then all was justified—murder, theft, lying, the forsaking of loyalties—anything and everything.

The television show garnered so much media attention that throughout the rest of the year, JZ became the object of television shows and countless newspaper and magazine articles, most overwhelmingly negative, most repeating the basic charges while adding some local twist. JZ provided a new occasion for articles when she published her autobiography in the fall of 1987. Her publicity tour made her readily available to the press. She was given a chance to answer her critics but at best was presented as an embattled hard-luck kid, on the defensive against some charges that had more truth, alluded the media, than she was willing to admit.

MORE ATTACKERS

And throughout 1987 several new voices were added to the attack. Some of the more extreme Christian counter-cultists who had begun targeting the New Age movement in the early 1980s finally discovered JZ and brought Ramtha into their version of the New Age Satanic movement then assaulting the Christian West. Texe Marrs, author of several anti–New Age texts, was alerted by an article that appeared in *USA Today* the same day the *20/20* show aired and branded Ramtha a demon being used by Satan to teach a laundry list of anti-Christian falsehoods. The following year he warned his readers to remember that the ram is a goat, and the goat is a long-established symbol of Satan.[3] His voice would be echoed by others, such as the vandals who painted "666" on the wall in front of JZ's home.

One expects deeply religious people to react from their theological opinions in a somewhat predictable manner. In like measure one also expects those ideological enemies of all things psychic to respond in a predictable manner, and Philip Haldeman of the Northwest Skeptics (the group networking with the Committee for the Scientific Investigation of the Paranormal) did not fail. He branded JZ and all her channeling colleagues as mere "power tripping frauds seeking fame and fortune." He offered his pop-psychological analysis of the students: They were people who possessed a deep, deep need to feel better; they have discovered "all this pseudoscientific nonsense about creating your own reality and loving yourself above all and never really dying is a lot more pleasant to deal with than reality."[4]

Yes, one can count on predictable, simplistic responses from the media, anti-cultists, and psychic cops; but with a serious researcher one expects something more. For example, in 1987 psychologist Jon Klimo published a book concerning his "investigations on receiving information from paranormal sources." Klimo made a rather empathetic survey of channeling and looked at a sampling of the channels who had become known either because they lived in the San Francisco Bay area where he worked or because their books and tapes were in local bookstores. He obviously had read many channeled texts and attempted to highlight strains of agreement he had discovered, noting similarities of insight across time and culture. He also provided a well-argued discussion of alternative, especially reductionist, approaches to understanding channeling. In the end he concluded,

> Channeling holds out to us the possibility of an incredibly complex, multi-leveled universe, filled with fellow consciousness, a universe with which we all interact in

new and meaningful ways, each of us taking ultimate responsibility for our respective growth. Rather than following some voice of authority from beyond ourselves, most of the channeled sources stress self-determination, guided from the highest levels within ourselves.[5]

And in discussing the channels he seemed, at times, to be acting as their public-relations agent. He presented them in the most positive light possible, even though their shady pasts were well known. For example, he discussed the case of the Fox sisters, the original Spiritualists, and their confessions of fraud as a case of sibling rivalry. He also highlighted the famous séance given by medium Arthur Ford to Episcopal Bishop James Pike on Canadian television, seemingly unaware that Ford and his control faked the séance. Ford's research notes for the event had been found among his papers shortly after his death in 1971 and fully discussed in the 1973 biography by the host of the television show on which the séance was given. Klimo also failed to mention the mentalism tricks to which Kevin Ryerson was prone and used to help convince Shirley MacLaine of his powers. Ryerson had been the student of one of the better mentalists of the latest generation, Richard Ireland.

Those examples notwithstanding, in the midst of the discussion of JZ and Ramtha, suddenly Klimo the investigator transformed into Klimo the rumormonger. Although negative rumors circulated in the Bay area New Age community about channels he discussed, he inserted the gossip about only one of them, JZ. He accused her of having been a former true channel who somehow had lost her original direction. He backed his assessment with a quote from the follower of another channel: "Many people now speculate that whatever energy came through J. Z. Knight has either shifted, departed or been replaced by a less benign entity."[6] To emphasize the point, he mentioned San Francisco's own Rev. Jim Jones (of the Jonestown massacre) into the text, thus branding JZ guilty by association.

JZ'S PROBLEMS

Only those closest to JZ knew that the adverse media coverage was the least of her problems. She was under intense financial pressure. The tax collector had joined the bill collectors in threatening to take everything. Actually, the strain of founding the school was almost a welcome distraction.

If that were not enough, while readers were learning of the whirlwind romance that had brought Jeff Knight into JZ's life, her family was becoming totally unraveled following the discovery of Jeremy's problems. Those problems would soon destroy her marriage and seriously challenge her confidence in life. Eventually, after her marriage to Jeff, he would take their cash reserve and leave her to face the bills alone. She would use much of her energy extricating herself from her dissolved relationship.[7] During interviews reporters perceived her feelings of hurt and discouragement. Not aware of the family situation, however, they concluded that it was due to insincerity and weakness (after all, true leaders have thick skins). Some of their questioning continued because they were unaware of her personal problems.

ANSWERING THE CRITICS

When I was contacted by JZ's lawyer and asked to be a witness in the court case brought by her former husband, I knew I would have to resolve to my satisfaction all the criticisms that had been leveled against the movement, no matter how superficial. Although I had monitored the movement for several years, I had read only a few books produced by the movement and had watched only one video, which I had shown to my classes. However, I had seen the *20/20* show and had a thick file of clippings on Knight/Ramtha. To prepare, I asked for books and tapes and the opportunity to visit the school and meet privately with the students. Everything I asked for was provided. For a month I came home early from work and listened to several hours of Ramtha, and I spent several weekends viewing Ramtha dialogues.

During my first trip to Yelm, I spoke with JZ. I toured the school, including the tank, and joined the students in fieldwork. Students I asked to interview became available at the next break. Linda Evans was pointed out to me. She had walked past several times, but I had not recognized her in scruffy clothes with her hair pinned back. I had a certain hesitancy in interviewing her; I know how hard it is for celebrities just to be people in their spiritual lives. We did have a brief conversation and I could not resist asking her about a tabloid article in which she was pictured with what appeared to be mud all over her face. The article suggested that she had been told by Ramtha to roll around in horse dung (which, given the number of horses at the ranch, is in great supply) and had obediently complied.[8] It seems that while filming a movie, she was thrown from a horse and landed in mud. Someone took her picture as she stood up and went to clean up. Then someone (she suspected but did not know who) gave the tabloid the picture and the story. We laughed about it, and she returned to her role as Ramtha's student.

144

My role in the lawsuit was to assess what was occurring at the school and to share with the court that information and my opinion on it. The numerous criticisms were secondary; in fact, most were not really criticisms at all but merely displays of political, theological, or philosophical rhetoric. For example, the accusation that the movement was Satanic was not really a criticism. Rather, it was a quick and most dramatic way the accusers communicated that they recognized Ramtha's teachings differed from those of Evangelical Christianity, that they disagreed with Ramtha's teachings, and that they were especially concerned that fellow Christians should shun Ramtha.

It is quite common in theological debate to express what is simply a personal disagreement by discussing a seemingly objective negative characteristic. Your opponent's opinion is wrong, outlandish, unbelievable. Statements of "I do not like it" become transformed into statements such as "It is wrong or bad." Those who complained, for example, that Ramtha had spoken through

JZ but had left and was replaced by a new entity or by JZ simply impersonating Ramtha are doing little more than describing their pilgrimages from belief to nonbelief. Rhetoric about mind control is primarily an expression of feeling threatened at creeping pluralism in a culture believed to be held together by some kind of religious homogeneity.

The case would be one of the last in the United States seriously to consider the issue of brainwashing. From my studies I had concluded that people use terms like *brainwashing* simply to communicate their disapproval of people who are enthusiastic followers of their religions and who persist in their faiths in spite of the opinions of nonbelievers. It had become fashionable for ex-members to explain their prior acceptance of a religious life as a result of brainwashing just as prior generations described themselves as being bewitched. Such an observation provides little information about the group. It does, however, offer the person speaking an opportunity to escape responsibility for prior choices, especially ones now believed to be mistaken. If I, a rational person, was really brainwashed or bewitched, then you can understand why I appeared to act and believe so foolishly in the past.[9]

But the question remained: Was JZ a fake? By the time I met her, she had recovered financially. (In fact, her former husband was suing for half her rebuilt estate.) As I observed Ramtha teaching, I could see nothing that immediately suggested fraud. So I began to query the students. They were intelligent, and they did not want to be duped or victimized by a con artist. They were reordering their lives around Ramtha's teachings. The older students, who knew JZ personally, had confronted the question and had resolved it to their satisfaction. They now understood clearly that JZ was one person and Ramtha quite another. They saw a radical difference between JZ—housewife and executive—and Ramtha—the Enlightened One. All shared stories of how they had gone through periods of questioning and close observation to test their eyes and ears. Linda Evans spoke with the greatest authority on this point. She came to Ramtha as a successful professional actress and was initially impressed with Ramtha's learning and erudition. But, as she told a reporter several years ago, "In the beginning I was totally suspicious. Being an actress and understanding acting, I wanted to see if this 'channeling' was trickery. I wanted to know if I could be fooled so that I could pro-tect myself."[10] She later confirmed to me that in all her years with Ramtha, she has never seen him break his persona: "If JZ is simply impersonating the Ramtha character, she is the greatest actress in the world. She should be in Hollywood where she would be at the top of the profession."

Evans was like most of the other long-term students. They had reached their understanding of Ramtha by a long, involved process. Before the school began, Ramtha's identity had been merely an academic question. JZ as Ramtha had been entertain-ing, had preached ideas with which they had agreed, and had made few demands upon their lives. At the school, however, they were asked to do increasingly "outrageous" things. They were taught C&E, were sent into the field with blindfolds, and were asked to sleep outdoors in their camping equipment for a week, sit with minimum clothing in freezing air, and walk in the tank for hours without a break. Some dropped out after each new chal-lenge. Those who stayed found that in doing those strange things, things they certainly would not have done on their own, they were growing, stretching their comfort limits, and discovering new insights about themselves. Their experiences were paying off (and rather quickly) in terms of new self-knowledge and new skills in facing the world. They trusted Ramtha. Following his teachings gave them what they had hoped to find.

And I found nothing that contradicted what Evans and the other students had told me. During the course of preparing this book I have spent more than sixty days in Ramtha's or JZ's pres-ence. For as much as a week at a time I spent hours listening to Ramtha teach, walked in the field as Ramtha observed his stu-dents' work, and, when opportunity was provided, spent the evenings informally in conversation with JZ, talking with her staff, or visiting with the people who work in her home. I have found nothing to suggest that she is anything other than who she says she is, the channel for a spirit entity named Ramtha. (Of course, who Ramtha is, is another question entirely.) I have on several occasions felt guilty when I reflected on my visits to Yelm. On the one hand, I worked hard building a relationship with JZ and spent much of my free time in the kitchen chatting with Molly Gordon, JZ's cook. On the other hand, almost every day I was there, without telling anyone I jumped back into my role of information gatherer and injected an issue into the conversation purely to observe reactions and to listen to the spontaneous response.

A MATTER OF HORSES

Having satisfied myself that JZ was sincere in what she was doing, I was ready to move on to what I saw as the more substantive criticisms that had been leveled at her. Few were more troublesome that what even JZ views as her worst mistake, at least in terms of the number of people it affected: her Arabian horse business. JZ had had a lifelong love of horses, and in the early 1980s she felt a great need for a recreational outlet from her daily routine, consumed as it was between her duties to her family and to Ramtha's as-yet-unarticulated mission. In 1982 she moved to the ranch at Yelm. The small town seemed an excellent place to raise Chris and Brandy (and the ranch would eventually become the site for Ramtha's school). Her impulsive purchase of a horse soon led to her buying one for each of her sons, and her meeting and falling in love with Jeff Knight gradually led to her involvement in the world of horse owners and horse shows.

147

She loved horses and had the money to indulge her habit. She went from owning a few horses to investing in the then-thriving Arabian horse trade. When, out of her own enthusiasm, she began to invite Ramtha's students into the business, did she not realize that some students who invested would make no clear separation between Ramtha and the woman who channeled him.

Suddenly, the bottom dropped out of the market. Not only did JZ go down, but she took a lot of people who, because of Ramtha, had trusted her.

In such a situation, saying "I'm sorry" is no response. But given her predicament, that was about all she could do. It is no wonder that many who lost money, along with their friends, bitterly left the movement. Only later was JZ able to act, and it is to her credit that she later realized what she had done and made restitution. It wasn't quick enough to undo all the damage, but eventually, as she recovered, she offered to make good everyone's losses.[11]

While fending off these criticisms, JZ also had to face criticisms of Ramtha's teachings. Many of Ramtha's critics agreed with JZ—she thought his philosophy outrageous when seen in the light of more conventional American religions—and found no better example in Ramtha's apparent granting of his students full permission to commit the most atrocious acts, including murder.

PERMISSION FOR EVIL?

If there has been a problem in communicating Ramtha's teachings, it has come when, like the Apostle Paul, he touches on the questions of sin and morality. Consider Ramtha's quotation:

> You know, God is lawless. Lawless! There are no laws in the Kingdom of God. Man is a law-abiding creature, but not God! The infinite spirit of your destiny is the flow of this Now and living it. And if your loins have a tremendous calling to do something, do something with them!

Having admonished the students to become lawless, he reiterated,

> Does not God love us enough to be all that we are, great and ugly, evil and divine? And hath He ever judged any of them to be either? No, He never has, entity, for you

are still here as a living testament of that truth. All of the things that you have ever desired in the purposeful darkness of your heart has *not* changed Life. So, you are still loved, regardless of what is in your Soul.

And what if your loins feel a calling to evil, maybe even murder?

[Murder, accidents, and robberies] are [the result of] contemplated experiences; they are not entrapments. They are created by the creator—You! They are not "forever" things; they are not "forever" circumstances. They are not "miseries" as a whole. In retrospect, they are great teachings.[12]

It sounds as if Ramtha is saying that moral law is of no use because faith alone is necessary for salvation. Because there is no law, all behavior is acceptable. If you murder someone, it's not a matter of great importance. Some have accused Ramtha that his teachings could lead his followers to commit crimes free from guilt. If ultimately there is no wrong, why not out of anger divorce your spouse, cheat your business partner, or kill your recalcitrant neighbor?

149

As with other religious teachings, one cannot take Ramtha's quotes, such as those just noted, remove them from the body of teachings in which they were offered, and suggest that they may lead to lawless behavior. Ramtha sees each person as an individualized divine being. That being is ideally free, a creator, but has become trapped in the world it created. Its task is to transcend the mundane world, realize its divine nature, and return to its divine status as an omnipotent divine creator. In the process of life, each individual has been many people, male and female, rich and poor, good and evil. Life and its rule are relative, the past merely prologue. Karma, the laws of society, and the rules of religions are all human creations. They do not participate in the basic structure of the universe. Having accepted the new definition of self as god and having experienced that reality in the training program, how, then, should students relate to society?

First, there is a theological response. Although Ramtha considers law, as do persons of many religions, to be a matter of the human realm rather than divine fiat, he does teach virtues natural to the gods, that is, to individuals. Love is such a virtue. Healing is a virtue. The ultimate goal is joy. A natural means to that joy is love of self.[13]

The natural activity of a self-loving god is creation, not destruction. An individual's return to the mode of life experience from before one discovered one's true nature would be self-contradictory and self-defeating, the means to even greater unhappiness. A god, in Ramtha's use of that term, is also a responsible self. In the process of self-realization of one's divinity, one must also accept responsibility for what one is, for what one chooses, and for one's behavior. I am responsible for my position in life. I am responsible for my decisions. I have no gripes coming. I will assume that my neighbors are also responsible persons. By my actions I call them to be responsible for themselves. That includes avoiding the role either of victim or victimizer.

Occasionally Ramtha speaks eloquently about students engaged in what he calls the Great Work in terms of its behavioral implications:

> And God, what about God? As you grow and mature you are going to learn that God is every living thing and that every person that you look upon, that God's hidden somewhere behind those eyes and that person has a destiny that they are not even aware that they have. And if only they could wake up and know that. How do you inspire that in other people? By living that yourself.
>
> Knowing God is the most sublime relationship of all, because it means that you set your goals back up the ladder. And why would you not want to learn how to heal

little children? And why would you not want to learn
how to forgive? And why would you not want to learn
how to manifest your dreams? Dreams, they are the seeds
of evolution. And why would you not want to learn how
to change? To know God is the highest principle of this
school, but to know God is to know yourself.[14]

Second, on a more pragmatic level, Ramtha teaches students
to be law-abiding and active in the community. JZ has expressed
her attraction to Cicero and his ideals of civic virtue, and she
has demonstrated those ideals by her involvement in the Yelm
community. Most well known is her college tuition scholarship
program for high school seniors, a charity that harks back to her
efforts to attend university. Less well known is her organizing effort
to feed people over the Christmas holidays. However, her civic
virtue is demonstrated more clearly in her involvement in county
environmental issues and her willingness to risk what has been a
fragile standing in Yelm by taking on local monied interests.

151

Ramtha's teachings call people to concentrate on remembering
their godhood. Although some realizations of that divinity come in
events at the school, the basic truths are understood only in daily
life: at work, at school, at play. If the teachings do not work there,
Ramtha's school is merely time out, an escapist paradise. Thus, students should demonstrate a better way to master life, not destroy it.

One aspect of the students' ethical stance was demonstrated
in their response to hostility precipitated by the *20/20* episode.
One rather humorous incident, which has attained a mythological status among students, occurred the day a local minister
organized a demonstration in front of the school. Students could
have ignored the happening (escapism) or could have showed
some righteous indignation (not altogether absent). The primary
response was neither. Instead, Ramtha led students outside to see
what was happening. They far outnumbered the demonstrators,
but there were no angry words, no attempt to shout down the
visitors. Following Ramtha's instructions, the students assumed

roles as observers and learned the worthlessness of being sucked into the vortex of the demonstrators' anger (which some soon turned on fellow picketers).

INTO THE FUTURE

Such has been the context in which Ramtha's School of Enlightenment has existed. Although no one has fed them to lions and no Inquisition has tortured them, students have been subjected to the modern equivalents because of a negative social environment created by a few people ideologically opposed to the school's teachings. The hostility, although it appears to be dying, crops up periodically. Most recently it came from articles in the national senior magazine *Modern Maturity* and from *Common Ground*, a New Age magazine serving the Northwest.[15]

The attacks have not slowed the school's development. The real damage has been personal. Whatever lessons have been learned, JZ and the students have felt wronged and defamed, held up to ridicule and called derogatory names by neighbors with whom they would like to live in harmony. They have been most concerned for their children, who have been verbally attacked at school. They have been angered by acts of violence and resentful of the time and energy given to frivolous lawsuits made possible because of the climate of prejudice generated by groups like the Cult Awareness Network. They look forward to a time when they can simply put this period behind them.

However, JZ and the school have realized some good from their situation. The period of hostility may, unintentionally, have assisted the school's development by keeping away all but the most highly motivated. The school draws most of its students from people previously identified with the New Age. It is likely that many more people would have flocked to the school had it not been for the rumors circulating within the movement and the public attacks.

On a more individual level, Ramtha has used the hostility as a teaching tool. In a hostile environment, students have had to confront not just their neighbors but what they do not like about themselves—all the personal baggage they bring to the school that is mirrored in the acrimonious remarks and the occasional spiteful action. Following an intense spiritual path creates a schoolroom in the most unexpected places.

In the United States there is a history of new groups going through a period of testing and controversy. In JZ's case, the controversy that makes Ramtha newsworthy also informs the public. In spite of the pain engendered, it allows those who reside in Yelm, as well as others who may never know or care very much about Ramtha and his school, to go about their business relatively sure that their town harbors neither a social cancer nor an evil cabal just waiting to reveal itself. Having attained that certainty, Ramtha's school and Yelm can look forward to a shared future from which both can benefit.

PARAPSYCHOLOGISTS COME TO YELM

Although I resolved any doubts I may have had about the sincerity of JZ and Ramtha, I still felt inadequate in describing what was occurring when Ramtha took the stage. Thus, while pursuing my research for this volume, I fantasized about having some direct parapsychological observation to supplement my work. I finally suggested to JZ that for her own enlightenment she might want to invite a parapsychologist to test her. I had one in mind: Stanley Krippner of Saybrook Institute, a former president of the Parapsychology Foundation for whom I had the greatest respect. After explaining to JZ what may happen, she gave her tentative agreement. It took a letter and several phone calls to convince Krippner to consider altering his research schedule. Finally, a meeting was arranged in the spring of 1996, out of which Krippner established a formal research program to be executed that summer.

Accompanying Krippner was a team of parapsychologists including Ian and Judy Wickramasekera and Ganapati Rao, an engineer from the University of Virginia (and later joined by

Charles W. Winstead and Ian Wickramasekera II). The team administered three psychological tests designed to test a subject's comfort level with dissociative states.[16] The Absorption Subscale of the Differential Personality Questionnaire has some ability to predict the ease with which the subject can enter an altered state of consciousness or produce psychophysiological changes in the body. The Dissociative Experience Scale measures the subject's frequency of dissociative experiences.

The Boundary Questionnaire measures the subject's psychological boundaries. It distinguishes between thin-boundaried people, characterized by such traits as openness, sensitivity, vulnerability, and ease at experiencing altered states of consciousness, and thick-boundaried people, who, in contrast, tend to be more structured and less open to change. They lead reliable, efficient, and well-organized lives, though they tend to be more rigid. Because they are less vulnerable, they are generally more capable of defending themselves when attacked, verbally or otherwise. They tend more to separate thought and feeling than do thin-boundaried individuals. In describing this test, Krippner emphasized that one type of personality was neither better nor worse than the other, just different.

JZ scored very high on the Absorption Subscale, indicating an ability to readily enter altered states of consciousness and to make changes in her body's psychophysiological state. She also scored high on the Dissociative Experience Scale, to be expected of someone who has lived much of her life in a dissociative state. Finally, also as may have been hypothesized, she tested as a very thin-boundaried person.

These tests also seem to predict the ease with which a person can enter altered states of consciousness and prepared the way for what turned out to be the more exciting phase of the testing. JZ allowed the team to monitor her while she went into and out of the trancelike state during which Ramtha appears. The team noted how rarely people like JZ make themselves available for such testing.

Monitoring was also the test about which JZ had the most hesitancy. Understandably, she felt uncomfortable being singled out as an experimental subject, not unlike a guinea pig. Also, the process of inviting Ramtha into her body partakes of the sacred; it had always been a very private matter. Those few who stay with her when she slips away make sure that when it is time for Ramtha to leave her body, JZ is in the same location as when Ramtha entered. Waking in the same location minimizes her personal disruption.

Testing of mediums dominated an era of psychical research. Researchers approached their subjects in the hope that the existence of spirit entities could be proven. That research was largely inconclusive. Many tests initially producing exciting results were later disproved; mediums had been trying to pull off the ultimate hoax by producing phenomena purporting to involve ectoplasm and materialization. Contemporary parapsychologists are more modest in their goals. Their tests stop short of proving the existence or credentials of paranormal entities. However, they can dispense with a variety of mundane explanations, the important ones being pathology and fraud.

The most intriguing questions to be asked concern Ramtha's independent existence. On the one hand, JZ insists that Ramtha exists independently of her and to that end testifies to being able to see him. Additionally, several students also claim to have seen him at least once. On the other hand, the great majority of people have had contact with Ramtha only when he manifests through JZ. His appearance, at least superficially, thus resembles various dissociative disorders. Many, including some former students, claim that it is simply acting on JZ's part.

To test these hypotheses, Krippner and the team monitored eight involuntary bodily functions, such as heart rate, muscle tension, pulse, skin temperature, and skin moisture, through an entire cycle. They began with JZ in her normal waking state with her eyes open. They then asked her to close her eyes for a time, after which she allowed Ramtha to enter her body. They then monitored her coming back to consciousness with her eyes both open and closed.

In reporting on these tests, Ian Wickramasekera noted the sudden, dramatic changes that accompanied Ramtha's move in and out of JZ's body. The heartbeat suddenly increased along with muscle tension and skin moisture while the pulse and skin temperature decreased. The tests were repeated on two later dates, with the same results. (Several students were also tested, with similar if less spectacular results.)

In reporting on these tests at a scholarly conference held at Yelm in February 1997, both Krippner and Wickramasekera agreed that the psychological patterns were so distinctive as to rule out fraud. There were no indications of pathology (multiple personality disorder). Thus, although the tests did not speak to the existence of Ramtha, they did rule out the two most common alternative theories: that JZ is offering a good stage performance or that she has a split personality.

In the end, the choice to believe in Ramtha constitutes a leap of faith. It's in the same category as believing in Jesus' resurrection or Muhammad's meeting with the angel. It is simply not the kind of question about which science is prepared to make authoritative pronouncements. However, because the questions of pathology and fraud were answered, nonbelievers will have to come up with more creative alternatives.

The results of the work of Krippner and his team were not available to me until after this book was largely completed, but it provided some added confirmation for some conclusions I had reached in my more mundane observations. I had found nothing to suggest that JZ was anything other than what she appeared to be, a channel who regularly went into a trancelike state during which time she gave over conscious control of her body to the entity Ramtha. While the relationship between JZ and Ramtha is, to say the least, a complicated one, it is not one that involves stage acting in which JZ essentially plays the part of Ramtha for an ignorant audience. Ramtha's students not only know this fact but have made the leap of faith to believe that Ramtha is also what he says he is, the Enlightened One. That leap of faith is regularly confirmed to them by their experience as they follow his instructions, strange as they might sometimes be. As long as Ramtha continues with the course he has pursued for the last decade, emphasizing the development of each student as a master, Ramtha should never lack for students to fill his unique School of Enlightenment.

157

EPILOGUE

ON STUDYING RAMTHA

During the last thirty years, I have devoted the bulk of my professional life to studying nonconventional, new religious movements. Yet, many colleagues were surprised when they learned I had chosen to engage in a study of Ramtha's School of Enlightenment. Some were merely asking why I chose Ramtha as opposed to the hundreds of other choices; others were challenging my choice, given Ramtha's unsavory reputation. For me the answer was simple. Having spent all my adult life observing spiritual organizations and metaphysical instructional centers, I saw in Ramtha's school a relatively new and unique offering, not only an alternative to older, more familiar forms of spirituality but also a decided challenge to New Age aspirations.[1] Additionally, over the last decade in particular, I had to admit to some degree of callousness developing. I thought I had seen it all. Each new group had its unique teaching or singular behavior pattern that set it apart, but the basic patterns were usually shared by several groups. Only rarely have I found someone doing something different.

Initially, I had no expectation of finding something unique from what the scholars of new religions had blandly classified as just another channeling group. They said that JZ Knight may be somewhat more successful than the average channeler, but essentially she was still simply a channeler presenting still another variation on the New Age message.

In the mid-1980s, JZ had become possibly the most successful of the New Age channels and had produced a particularly useful tape describing the process of entering the trance state and channeling, which I used in my classes at the University of California. But then, in the late 1980s, all of a sudden she disappeared. I took passing note because I was writing the *New Age Encyclopedia*. However, I had assumed, as has come to pass, that the New Age was an ephemeral happening and that as it disintegrated it would splinter into more in-depth movements. I concluded that Ramtha's followers had merely separated themselves from the larger New Age world to attend to his truths. I was right as far as I went, but I was not prepared for what I found when I finally visited Yelm.

160

Far beyond my immediate consultation duties in Yelm, I became excited by what I saw. As a chronicler of American religion, I realized that here was a welcome change from New Age pablum and endless inspirational pep talks. I worked hard that week (I had to explain to a judge in simple terms what was going on at the school), but I was motivated more by having discovered a fresh blossom on the tree of American religious pluralism. (I know it sounds weird, but all scholars get their kicks by finding something that would bore most people to tears.)

It has been a while since I wrote something other than either a conference paper or a reference book that was put together nonlinearly as so many pieces of information. However, dusting off some rusty writing skills was not nearly as difficult as dealing with basic personal, intellectual, and moral issues raised by the study, issues I felt I had handled sufficiently many years ago but that came back in full force as I pursued my observation of Ramtha. The issues were raised by the distinctly different hats I wear: first, as a United Methodist minister with a deep commitment to conservative Evangelical Protestantism; and second, as a scholar attempting to understand new alternative religious movements and who enjoys and appreciates his association, however informal, with a modern, secular, state-supported university.

In those moments when I donned my ministerial hat, I had to resist the temptation to engage Ramtha in a theological critique, though I could not resist adding some reflections calling attention to the often radical distinctions between the school's teachings and traditional Christian theology. There is no denying that Ramtha's theology raised a host of personal questions for me. Since graduate school I have felt that Gnosticism has been the great and important alternative teaching against which Christianity has struggled. The second-century church demonstrated its integrity by carrying on a polemic warfare with the Gnostics in its midst at a time when it not only lacked state power to implement its decisions but also needed all the friends it could get just to survive Rome's actions against it. I also agreed with the many commentators who have seen Gnosticism creeping back into the Protestant church, the result of pietistic trends attempting to fill the spiritual vacuum in congregational life decimated by a liberal Protestant theology that, to a large extent, neglected the nurturing of personal religion. Gnosticism is the constant temptation to those going through a period of dryness in spirituality or alienation from community.

I was initially introduced to the Gnostics by my patristics professor who happened to be a specialist in Gnosticism. But neither of us ever expected to see a functional Gnostic school, and we had little idea what it would look like. And as I sat in on the classes at Ramtha's school, I also remembered discussions that followed the emergence of the Charismatic movement in the 1970s. Was the speaking in tongues, healing, and prophetic activity we observed like those in the early church? Could we legitimately view the Charismatic movement as a modern equivalent by which to understand early Christianity? Now new versions of the questions occasionally forced their way into consciousness: Is Ramtha's school actually a doorway into the past? Will studying Ramtha provide a new perspective on the ancient Gnostics?

My Evangelical colleagues have most clearly understood the rise of Gnosticism. But they are also the ones who, in their hasty and often inappropriate branding of many divergent theologies as Gnostic or pantheistic, have to a certain extent allowed the term *Gnostic* to be transformed into a pejorative label with little descriptive value. That polemic use of the term is due to a certain laziness on our part. In examining alternative systems of thought, we quickly see their differences from Christianity and quite naturally want to find a label that will provide a shortcut to our categorizing them. After all, average church members do not want to know about different movements in any detail. They desire only simple answers to key questions: What's wrong with them? and Why should I (and my offspring) stay away from them?

My encounter with many Evangelical Christians who write about other religions has, to some extent, helped shape my life's work. However, over the years I have been mostly disappointed with the Christian writing in this area. Instead of attempting to understand the teachings of a group, too frequently writers only compared quotes from the group's literature with biblical passages, both often out of context. Then, as I began to visit the groups, I often encountered the anger at the church many members had because of Christian writers who had written supposedly authoritative books but who had distorted members' positions and had condemned them for believing things they had never taught. In most cases the writer had never visited them and had relied solely on either the word of ex-members or on one or two pieces of literature. Such superficial consideration not only misrepresented a group's beliefs and practices but failed to grasp the religion's essential appeal to the hearts and the heads of individuals on religious quests.[2]

I have always thought the church deserved better, and many years ago I committed myself to providing it with the information it needed both to live at peace with its new neighbors and to carry on its missional life with a high level of integrity. I also encouraged young scholars who wanted to work in the field and have been positively ecstatic over the number who have chosen to devote the major part of their research time to the study of noncoventional religions. It is out of that underlying vocational choice that this work should be understood by my Christian colleagues. Our neighbors who have different beliefs should first be understood and appreciated, for they are our neighbors, not some sinister unknown growing as a parasite on the community. If, after we understand them and come to know them as human beings, we still have a problem with their theology or their behavior, we have a context in which to present our issues. We do not serve the cause of Christ by branding people of other faiths as followers of Satan or by speaking to them in tones so filled with anger and hate that the words of love can never be heard.

I took as the mandate for my study of Ramtha my decision to spend my life documenting and trying to understand the pluralistic religious life I saw around me. Vocationally, the most influential force in my life was the writings of a man I never met but who became my hero, Elmer T. Clark. Clark had given his life to the Methodist Church in the South where I was raised. He was an executive with the mission board during most of that time. Along the way he wrote a classic in the psychology of religion, *The Psychology of Religious Awakening*, and devoted his later years to writing on Methodist history. He compiled an immense library that, on his death, went to the United Methodist Church archive.

163

While my contemporaries became enthused with UFOs, Elvis Presley, or Alabama football, during my last year in high school one of Clark's books, *The Small Sects in America*, captured my imagination. After reading it I wanted to consume everything written on American alternative religions. And from my reading I concluded, among other things, that the comprehensive account of the history and life of a new religious movement, especially one around which a public controversy had swirled, was far more interesting and complicated than the few facts reported in the press or the charges leveled by ex-members.

Most reporters are not interested in that comprehensive a story. They work on deadlines and have to get the news, and news seems to be little more than reporting a rumor of wrongdoing or an account of some bizarre activity. Ex-members, even those with righteous complaints, tend to reconstruct their experiences— ambiguous situations at worst—into totally negative encounters. They tend to demonize the leaders and turn the members into zombielike followers. Harmless comments are recast into sinister threats, group jargon into conspiratorial fantasies. When charges, rumors, and half-truths are flung at the community, they become like feathers in the wind: extremely hard to catch. I did not mention every charge that has circulated about Ramtha, but I acknowledged the more important ones and provided a context out of which some understanding of the charges can be better understood.

With the easing of the cult wars that raised the study of new religions from the fringe to its proper place in religious studies, a final reason for this work became evident. Given the number of scholars of new religions who have appeared in the last generation, it is unfortunate that of the six hundred to one thousand new religions, a few controversial ones have been overstudied and a few have been given limited observation, but the majority have been shown no scholarly interest. Ramtha's School of Enlightenment has been one of the latter groups in spite of its well-recognized success, the large amount of literature it has published, and the controversy surrounding it.

Ramtha's school typifies the group scholars generally neglect. First, it differs radically from most groups studied in that it is not a youth religion. Its greatest appeal has not been to young adults so much as it has to people in their thirties and forties who are ready to make a second transition in their lives. Thus, it has none of the youthful characteristics (or problems) associated with groups such as the Unification Church or the Hare Krishna movement. Further exploration of similar groups will provide a welcome corrective to limited theoretical approaches to new religions based solely on some of the youth groups.

Second, Ramtha's school is an esoteric school, meaning that many of its teachings, including most of its important ones, are

not generally presented to outsiders. Even advanced students sitting in on a beginning event are admonished not to practice
advanced disciplines in the presence of the newer students. Such
secrecy can be an obstacle but in most cases not a permanent
barrier. As I discovered when I researched magic and witchcraft
in the early 1980s, most esoteric groups are happy to welcome an
outside scholar and will even allow participation in their most
private rites and worship. However, the scholar will have to
spend some time building group trust and understanding the
worldview within which the rites and practices gain their logic.
Most important, the scholar must be careful to respect the group
and not violate the group's sense of the sacred.[3]

Third, Ramtha's school is an esoteric Gnostic school. Many
scholars have been attracted to the study of Eastern groups or
Christian revivalist groups. Western Gnostic groups, even with
the attention given the New Age movement, remain a lesser concern. That lack is one of the basic distortions in the literature.
Although the Unificationists and Krishnas claim tens of thousands, the New Age movement and esoteric traditions claim
(literally) millions. Most communities in America have never
seen a Unification mobile team, Hare Krishnas doing *kirtan*, or a
Scientology auditor. But more than 20 percent of the American
public profess a belief in astrology, and several million have formally associated themselves with the New Age milieu and are
now affiliated with one of its many components. Thus, although
Ramtha's School of Enlightenment may itself be relatively small,
it is the symbol of a major alternative trend in Western religious
life: the rise of a new Gnosticism.

It is my hope that this volume will encourage other studies
of Gnostic and related groups in their particularity, not just as
additional components of the large amorphous New Age milieu.
Inhibited by the varied names under which modern Gnosticism
has flourished, we are only beginning to trace the rise of this
major form of alternative Western spirituality in a manner that
integrates our knowledge into the larger considerations of the

emerging worldwide pluralistic religious culture. The revival of Gnosticism ranks with the rise of Islam and the influx of Eastern religions as among the most significant changes in Western religion in the twentieth century.

APPENDIX

ANCIENT GNOSTICISM

In claiming the name *Gnostic* for Ramtha's School of Enlightenment, JZ Knight has placed Ramtha's teachings in the lineage of the major alternative religious tradition in the West. Gnosticism, like Christianity, originated in the ancient Mediterranean Basin and emerged onto the historical stage in the second century A.D. when its proponents began a lengthy struggle with Christians for hegemony over Europe. The church won, and although one Gnostic group, the Manichaeans, spread eastward across Asia as far as China, Western Gnosticism was reduced to a footnote in Christian history and most of its ancient writings presumed lost. As modern critical historical research developed, the major sources for understanding Gnosticism were the Christian books that had inadvertently preserved fragments of Gnostic writings in the process of refuting the Gnostic position.

Then in 1947–1948, at about the same time as the discovery of the Dead Sea Scrolls, a library of Gnostic texts was discovered in Egypt, preserved over the centuries by the dry desert environment. Recognized and published, these scrolls from Nag Hammadi, in the Nile River Valley northwest of Luxor, provided

a more complete understanding of Gnosticism's theological perspective and an appreciation of its importance in the ancient
world. The scolls also allowed scholars to recognize and assemble
texts produced throughout the centuries that drew from the early
Gnostic teachings. Integrating archeological finds left by Asian
Gnostic communities with information from the Mandeans, the
single surviving ancient Gnostic community in Iran, provided
additional insight. It was finally possible to construct a history of
Gnostic thought from the ancient world to the present.

THE BEGINNINGS OF GNOSTICISM

The discovery of the Nag Hammadi library intensified the debate
over the origins of Gnosticism, especially as it related to
Christianity. Did Gnosticism develop within Christianity, or did
it have an independent origin and develop a relationship with
the church as Christianity spread throughout the Mediterranean
Basin? There are good arguments on both sides. However, there
are signs in the New Testament of at least an early form of what
would appear as full-blown Gnostic systems.[1]

Although Gnosticism appears to have pre-Christian roots,
by the second century it was alive and well. It became visible
within the church as a set of tendencies and alternative ideas,
condemned by writers whose books were later compiled into the
New Testament. The church then became engaged in an intense
struggle against Gnostic teachers. In his antiheretical writings,
Bishop Irenaeus condemned those Gnostics who had absorbed
much of the language of Christianity but who offered a consider-
ably distinct perspective on God, salvation, and the cosmos.[2]

In the basic Gnostic myth, of which there were numerous
variations, the universe originated as the harmonious emanation
from the True God of the heavenly realm. That realm was popu-
lated with the Aeons, the eternal beings, representatives of the
eternal essences of God. God resides in the abyss of silence
unknowable by words, and yet some knowledge of God can be

derived by reference to the Aeons. According to the Valentinians, one of the more important Gnostic sects, the highest Aeons are Intellect (nous) and Truth. Also close to God, but not as close as Intellect, are the Word (Logos) and Life. Other Aeons are Faith, Hope, Love, and Unity. The Aeons populate the several levels of the heavenly realm. To the believers, the Aeons delineated a hierarchy of virtues pictured as most godlike.

In the Valentinian myth, only the Intellect, the Son, understood God perfectly.[3] The other Aeons wished to know God as directly as Intellect did but were hindered by God's remoteness. Then Aeon Sophia (Wisdom) developed an intense desire to know God and in her eagerness moved toward God but made her move without bringing along her companion. She thereby became guilty of wrong, and by her action a flaw came into existence. Sophia (or, by some accounts, an aspect of her) was tossed out of (or fell from) the heavenly realm. In her debased state, because of her prior intention to know God she gave birth to the Demiurge, an inferior being who was an imperfect image of the True God.

The Gnostic system presented a double creation: the creation of the heavenly realms (including the souls of humans) and the creation of our physical world, which resulted from the single flaw that appeared in the heavenly realms. The Demiurge (or Artisan) is so named because he was responsible for fashioning this world. He was identified as the creator God pictured in the Old Testament. The God of the Bible is thus seen as a lesser image of the True God, and, in like measure, this world is a distorted model of the heavenly realm.

The Demiurge, a being who first appears in Plato's writings, became a central figure in the Valentinian myth. He operated through seven beings, called archons or angels, whom he created and who cooperated with him. According to one explanation of human creation, the Demiurge fashioned the physical world, including the human body. But in his attempt to give vitality to humans, he breathed life into them. That breath carried the divine light that Sophia had passed to him from the heavenly realm.

Thus, humans are divine beings of the heavenly realm but are trapped in bodies of matter, bodies fashioned by the Demiurge.

The Demiurge wished to be acknowledged as the True God and to rule the human soul. He fashioned the law as a tool of his rulership. Humanity was caught by the ignorance of its true nature. Although the specific manner in which humans came to be entangled in this world varied from one Gnostic teacher to another, the end product was the same: because of ignorance humans cannot recover their divine birthright in the higher realms.

To save humanity, Intellect or Word descended from the heavenly realm and revealed to humans the truth of their origin and destiny. To deliver this teaching, Intellect, identified with the Christ, descended upon Jesus at the time of his baptism and from that time forward spoke through Jesus and revealed the truth of human nature. The Christ departed at the time of Jesus' death and returned to heaven. Although Jesus suffered, died, and was resurrected, the Christ, a spiritual being, could neither suffer nor die. For the Gnostics, Christ was not the title of Jesus the Savior but a separate divine being distinct from Jesus.

The separation between Christ and Jesus symbolizes a distinction that runs throughout Gnosticism and draws a strict distinction between the real spiritual world and the visible created world, between spirit and matter, between soul and body. In some systems the material world is denigrated; it is evil. In others it is only a lesser reality, evil only because it is the place in which the divine souls of people are trapped. But plainly, Gnosticism led to a lower opinion of the material world, often accompanied by a withdrawal from mores such as social order and the law. Gnostics tended to become either ascetics and renunciates (because the visible material world was evil) or libertines (because action in the world is ultimately irrelevant).

Gnosticism matured into a complete alternative to biblical Christianity. It can be identified by several characteristic ideas, including the following:

1. God is remote, impersonal, and unknowable and is most closely identified with the attributes of the Aeons, representatives of the eternal essences of God, which fill the heavenly realm.

2. The world originated by hierarchical radiation (emanation) rather than by an act of creation by a personal deity. Thus, the universe exists in layered divisions, the higher levels being more spiritual and closer to God, the lowest level being that of the physical world. Salvation involves the knowledge of and the ability to traverse the levels.

3. God is not responsible for the material world or for the mundane social order. Both are seen either as evil or at best as only somewhat good, having no ultimate relevance to humanity's salvation or destiny.

171

GNOSTICISM SPREADS

These ideas, adapted into a variety of systems, were passed from one generation to the next. In the third century they would be molded to fit the dualism of Manichaeism and Mandaeanism.[4] After Christianity gained control of the Roman Empire, Manichaeism was persecuted as a heresy, but took refuge in the Islamic lands and in the Balkans as Bogomilism, where it survived for several centuries. Toward the end of the first millennium it spread into central Asia, where it thrived until the Mongol invasions of the thirteenth century. Manichaeans were reported in China as late as the seventeenth century. Mandaeanism has survived somewhat tenuously in southern Iraq and Iran to the present. As of the 1970s, the Mandaean community numbered approximately 14,000, but current figures are unavailable. Not only have many migrated, but their homeland became a battleground in both the Iran-Iraq War (1980–1988) and the Iraq-Kuwait conflict (1990–1991).

Gnostic tendencies constantly reappeared in church theological controversies as the church evolved into the dominant medieval religious institution in the Middle Ages. Gnosticism was the perennial temptation for the mystics and periodically reemerged in strength as organized religious communities. For example, the Paulician movement, which first appeared in the seventh century in Armenia, was a new version of Manichaeism. Although the movement renounced any tie to Mani, the founder of Manichaeism, it retained most of his doctrines. The Paulicians believed that the Christ attached himself to Jesus prior to his birth. Jesus was said to have passed through the body of the Virgin like water through a pipe, a belief the church saw as most insulting to the Virgin Mary. The disparagement of matter as evil led the Paulicians to consider baptism a purely spiritual matter, and they rejected the practice of the Lord's Supper.

The Byzantine government attempted to stamp out the spread of the Paulician movement, but persecution merely spurred further growth. Persecution continued periodically through the eleventh century, by which time the center of the movement had shifted to the southern Balkans, most notably Bulgaria and Bosnia. There, in the fifteenth century the Muslims overran the Paulician communities, but they survived until the Ottoman Muslims were driven back to Turkey. Efforts to convert the Paulicians occurred as late as the seventeenth century, and dualistic sects are still reported to exist in the southern Balkans, though the connection between these present-day sects and the Paulicians has not been firmly established.

A dualistic Gnosticism emerged along the French-Italian border in the twelfth century. Originally called Cathari, believers were eventually named Albigensians for the town of Albi in the Languedoc district, where a council was called to mobilize forces against them. The Albigensians seemed to have Paulician roots, Paulicians having been active in Italy as early as the seventh century. The destruction of the Albigensians in the mid–thirteenth century forms one of the bloodiest episodes in the history of the Roman Catholic Church and the Inquisition.[5]

THE KABBALAH

Although Gnosticism persisted in Christian form in groups such as the Paulicians and Albigensians, it also found a new home within the Jewish community as the Kabbalah. Scholars disagree over its origins, some tracing it to the Babylonian (Iraq) Jewish community. Whatever the beginning, the developing thought was written in the *Book of Zolar* in the thirteenth century by Moses de Leon (1250–1305). In this form it circulated in Jewish communities throughout Europe. Possibly earlier was the *Sepher Yesirah* (Book of Creation).

The Kabbalah (variously spelled cabala, quabalah, qabala, etc.), a Hebrew word meaning "doctrines received from tradition," proposes the emanation of the world from God, the Ein Soph. God is the preexistent One, about Whom nothing can really be said. However, it is proper to speak of the Ein Soph becoming active and creative and having as the instrument of that creation the *sephiroth*, the divine emanations. The first sephiroth, Kether, was simply the wish to become manifest. Each sephiroth in turn produced another, until ten appeared, the last, Malkuth, being the manifest world. The ten sephiroth are pictured as the tree of life (see figure 6), with Kether at the top and Malkuth at the bottom. Like the Aeons of the ancient Gnostics, each sephiroth represented an ideal virtue or quality inherent in the Ein Soph. They are as follows:

173

1. Kether (Crown)	beingness, existence
2. Chochmah	wisdom
3. Binah	intelligence, understanding
4. Chesed	mercy, love
5. Geburah	strength, severity, justice
6. Tiphareth	beauty
7. Netzach	firmness
8. Hod	glory
9. Yesod	foundation
10. Malkuth	kingdom

Figure 6. The Kabbalistic Tree of Life

Some presentations of the Kabbalah include an eleventh sephiroth, Daath, concealed between and behind Chochmah and Binah. Daath refers to knowledge (of the sexual kind) and often plays a prominent role in modern sex magick systems.

After the tree of life was constructed, it was capable of almost infinite expansion to include all the phenomena anyone could encounter. For example, the tree was seen as a model of a human. It existed as the heavenly primordial man (and is in its presentation quite literally sexist), of which the human body is a mere shadow. If it is placed on the picture of a human body, Kether is at the head and Malkuth at the feet. The three triangles in the tree can be seen as the triads of intellectual (existence, wisdom, intelligence), moral (love, justice, beauty), and physical (firmness, glory, foundation) virtues or qualities.

The tree could be multiplied into four worlds, each consisting of a complete tree, the first being the world of the heavenly man, the direct emanation of the Ein Soph. From it is produced the world of creation, the *briatic* world, inhabited by the angel Metatron. Next appears the less refined world of formation, the *yetziratic* world, the abode of angels. Finally the world of matter and action comes. Humanity begins its existence in this realm.

175

If the four layers and ten sephiroth were not enough, each sephiroth could contain a complete tree. Each sephiroth was connected to other sephiroths by lines or paths. The paths related the virtues to one another, thus opening a new line of philosophical exploration. Path-working is a popular discipline of the modern occult Kabbalist.

With the Kabbalah, we have for the first time a complete Gnostic system to examine. The adoption of the Kabbalah by a segment of the Jewish community and its subsequent discovery by the first generation of Protestant scholars (who were learning Hebrew as they attempted to bypass Latin and return to the original language of the Bible) brought the Kabbalah more exposure and assured its survival—as well as its debasement by amateurs.

However, we can see in the Kabbalah a way of organizing the world through an intense system of personal exploration and development, providing a logical structure of moral development that leads to mystical experience. The system begins with Malkuth, the mundane world that must be mastered before any real progress in the other sephiroth can be made. It was a tradition that one should not begin the study of Kabbalah until one's fortieth year, because one had to master one's environment and gain the experience of life. However, as one began to work along the paths and to ever higher sephiroth, several methods became available ranging from the magical to the mystical, the active to the passive and emphasizing concentrated will or contemplation (though usually a little of both). Along the way, as in any mystical system giving significant attention to the inner life, psychic phenomena and communication with spirit entities (angels and demons) offered themselves as enticements to further growth and as distractions to the ultimate quest.

The Kabbalah enjoyed its greatest era beginning in the eighteenth century as the Hassidic (Jewish mystical sect) movement spread throughout the large Jewish communities of eastern Europe. The group in each country developed its lineages of teachers around an original great teacher or rebbe, usually revered for his exemplifying great sanctity, intellectual accomplishments, and miracle-working abilities. The Hassidim thrived until their communities were mostly destroyed in the Holocaust. Fortunately, a few rebbes were able to escape and continue their work in America and Israel.

In the nineteenth century the Kabbalah, which had been mostly dropped by later generations of Protestant scholars, was rediscovered by a former Catholic-seminarian-turned-occultist, Alphonse-Louis Constant, known by his kabbalistic pen name, Éliphas Lévi (1810–1875). Lévi saw in the Kabbalah a tool for the revival of magic, which tied together the tarot, numerology, and the spirit invocation.

The Kabbalah reaches into the ancient past, but in its refined form has survived as an active system in the contemporary world.

It possesses all the characteristics of the ancient gnosis (wisdom). God is remote, indescribable, impersonal, existing beyond the cate-gories of language. Even the idea of existence would limit the Ein Soph. The world comes into existence by hierarchical emana-tion—the spiritual to the less spiritual to the material. The world of the ten sephiroth closely resembles the realms of the Aeons through which humanity's spiritual aspect must pass to return to its origin in the heavens. Salvation comes by an inner process of devel-opment and attainment. The mundane world must be mastered, but only as a step toward leaving it behind.

In spite of the knowledge the ancient texts offer of Gnostic cosmology, scant attention is given to the practical side of Gnostic life. What did Gnostics do to attain their mystical goals? No system of practice was discussed, though various rituals, including baptismal rites, were known. Sexual intercourse was integral to some groups. However, just as there was a general denigration of the material, visible world, so there was a turning away from ceremony and worship as commonly practiced, includ-ing the need for regular ceremonies such as the Lord's Supper or mass. A personal deity accepts worship; an impersonal deity has no need of it.

With Kabbalah, our knowledge of the practice emerges. Hassidic schools combine the study of text, ecstatic dance, life with the rebbe, and prayer and contemplation to produce the mystical life. As adopted by magicians, the Kabbalah provides a framework for magical practices appropriate to the level of attainment—ritual, psychic development, invocation, guided meditation, and con-scious image making (active imagination) being primary tech-niques. Israel Regardie speaks of the processes of Kabbalistic ceremonial magic being the Western form of yoga, a disciplined form of inner exploration leading to mystical attainment.[6]

Gnosticism thus survived in its variant forms across Europe, though in the Catholic West it was constantly threatened when-ever it attracted the church's attention. The Inquisition developed into a well-oiled machine fighting the Albigensians but then turned its attention to other social dissidents. Eventually it would attack the problem of witchcraft.

The antiwitchcraft crusade began in the 1480s; however, its fury was checked by two other imminent problems. First, Islam had invaded Europe from Turkey by way of the Danube River valley, had overrun Budapest, and threatened Vienna. Second, in the north demands for reforming the decadent church erupted into the Protestant Reformation. The Muslims were stopped at Vienna, but Protestantism took over into Great Britain, Germany, Scandinavia, parts of Switzerland, and, eventually, Holland. Although Roman Catholics placed the problems of protecting its western flank from Islam and the new reality of a divided Christendom at the top of its priorities, Protestants and Catholics found a common cause in attacking people they labeled witches. Meanwhile, a radical new form of Gnosticism quietly appeared—alchemy.

178

ALCHEMY AND ITS HEIRS

Some science textbooks still treat alchemy as a precursor to chemistry, a kind of proto-chemistry carried on by prescientific intellectuals still playing children's games in their laboratories. After all, what can one do in a laboratory if there is no understanding of the elements, atomic structure, and the basic building blocks of scientific methodology? We now know that our understanding of alchemy has been shaped by an era that worshipped science and its accomplishments and had little or no understanding of what was considered the silly superstitions of the occult.

The occult revival has provided a new context in which to return to the alchemical texts, which make no sense at all if read scientifically, especially if we are attempting to reconstruct experiments to make gold or produce the elixir of life. We go on a foolish quest in search of the philosopher's stone if we hope to one day wear it as a necklace.

Alchemy was an attempt to create a new Gnostic system using what was then scientific language as a code for philosophical and religious speculations. We can comprehend this intent from the early alchemical teachers. Nicolas Valois, for example, noted, "The good God granted me this divine secret through my prayers and the good intentions I had of using it well; the science is lost if purity of heart is lost." Heinrich Khunrath advised the young alchemist to "Pray theosophically and work physio-chemically." Thus, the Comte de Buffon, one of the founders of modern science, complained, "It must be admitted that nothing can be got from books on alchemy. Neither the *Table hermétique*, the *Tourbe des Philosophes*, nor Philalethes and various others whom I have taken the trouble to read and even study seriously, have offered me anything but obscurities and unintelligible processes."[7]

Alchemy seems to have emerged in the thirteenth century in the writings of Nicolas Flamel, who claimed he had developed his ideas from a book by one Abraham, a Jew.[8] The alchemical texts, usually illustrated with elaborate symbolic drawings, describe the Great Work, the process of changing the dross of the human soul into the refined gold of the enlightened heavenly man. The illustrations make little sense as pictures of mundane realities (scientific or otherwise) but make perfect sense as a Gnostic system of inner development. Basile Valentin, writing in the mid-1600s, presented a picture of a man carrying the universe. Around him waved a banner with the Latin phrase *Visita Interriota Terra Rectificando Invenies Occultum Lapidem*. The phrase translates, "Visit the inner parts of the earth, by rectification thou shalt find the hidden stone," a clear invitation to inner exploration. However, equally interesting today is the word spelled with the first letter of each word on the banner: VITRIOL. Vitriol was a common substance we know as sulfuric acid. However, the corrosive vitriol known to past ages was not what the young alchemist needed.

Alchemy was able to survive and flourish, among intellectuals at least, at the same time that witchcraft trials were tearing apart the body politic. Alchemists were able to play the intellectual games by covering their philosophical quests in seemingly scientific endeavors. Popular misunderstandings were boosted by

179

charlatans who claimed abilities to produce gold for financially strapped rulers or the elixir of life for a public afflicted by all kinds of illnesses. Few took the trouble to read the texts in which frequently the secret was given away. As Valois said of the philosopher's stone, "It is a Stone of great virtue and is called a Stone, and is not a stone."[9] Other texts speak of a "true mercury" of which the common metal is only a bastard son.

In alchemy the Kabbalistic tree of life is replaced with a furnace, generally pictured as an upright structure whose inward area is divided into levels, usually three. One seventeenth-century manuscript provided a list of alchemical operations as purgation, sublimation, calcination, exuberation, fixation, solution, purification, and fermentation leading to the elixir.

Alchemy is of vital importance because it operated when Roman Catholics and, later, Protestants were most interested in suppressing rival theologies. Alchemy declined throughout the seventeenth century and almost disappeared in the eighteenth, part of the general transition of occult thought from older, supernatural models to newer, scientific ones. Its reputation, besmirched by the new scientists of the eighteenth century, would give way to the new modern occultism of the Rosicrucians and the speculative world of Freemasonry.[10]

Alchemy carried the Gnostic tradition through the Middle Ages. Yet, it was plainly the tradition of a few, some the most learned of European intelligentsia, several the most clever of rogues. In spite of a most intolerant ruling elite, they were able to play the game required to pursue their studies and communicate with their colleagues. Their coded language could inform those on the inside where their speculations had taken them while convincing the uninitiated that they were merely discussing subjects of no great import to theology, certainly no challenge to orthodoxy. One of the more interesting paradoxes of that era was that while the Inquisition hunted out the practitioners of magic in villages throughout Europe, the kings and queens invited alchemists into their midst as honored guests.

Appendix

THE REDISCOVERY OF HERMES

Adding depth to the body of alchemical texts in the late medieval period was the rediscovery of Hermes Trismegistus (Thrice-Greatest Hermes), an ancient Egyptian writer. Some thought of him as a contemporary of Moses; others believed him to be the incarnation of Thoth (or Tehuti), the Egyptian god of learning, because Hermes is the Greek name of Thoth. Hermes, however, seems to be the name used by several writers who shared a similar worldview, all ascribing their work to the ancient Egyptian master. Although the writings of Hermes were known in the early Middle Ages, they were ignored because they were believed to have been written by students of the Greek philosopher Plotinus (204–270 A.D.).

The texts survive only in their Greek translations and purport to be from the period of the Greek conquest of Egypt, when they were copied from the ancient Egyptian texts believed to be in the hands of the priesthood. The Hermetic texts, rather than bearing the stamp of Egyptian origin, however, seem to be in the lineage of Greek Platonic philosophy. Although some may be as early as the first century B.C., they seem to have been written over a period up to the third century A.D. It is also likely that many of them were lost, as were so many ancient texts that existed in only a few copies. What is important for our purposes is that a Latin translation by Ficinus of the surviving Hermetic texts was published in 1471, and in 1554 an edition of the original Greek texts was published by Turnebus. The texts were subsequently republished on several occasions throughout the sixteenth century, during the period when Europe was convulsed by the separation of much of northern Europe and England from the Roman Catholic fold.

Ficinus's translations provoked widespread interest in the Hermetic writings, and eight editions appeared before 1500. An additional sixteen editions appeared throughout the first half of the 1600s. Of these texts, the first, the *Poimandres*, is the most important because upon it the later Hermetic tradition would largely draw its sustenance. However, in 1541 a Latin translation

181

of the most famous Hermetic document appeared. This brief work, *The Emerald Tablet*, named because it was thought to have been originally inscribed in Phoenecian on emerald stone, summarized the Hermetic vision:

> True, without error, certain and most true; that which is above is as that which is below, and that which is below is as that which is above, for performing the miracles of the One Thing; and as all things were from the one, by the mediation of one, so all things arose from this one by adaptation; the father of it is the Sun, the mother of it is the Moon; the wind carries it in its belly; the nurse thereof is the Earth. This is the Father of all perfection, or consummation of the whole world. The power of it is integral, if it be turned into earth. Thou shalt separate the earth from the fire, the subtle from the gross, gently with much wisdom; it ascends from earth to heaven, and again descends to earth; and receives the strength of the superiors and of the inferiors so thou hast the glory of the whole world; therefore let all obscurity flee before thee. This is the strong fortitude of all fortitudes, overcoming everything subtle and penetrating every solid thing. So, the world was created. Hence were all wonderful adaptations of which this is the manner. Therefore am I called "Thrice-Greatest Hermes," having the Three Parts of the Philosophy of the whole world. That which I have written is consummated concerning the operation of the sun.[11]

182

The phrase "as above, so below" became the cornerstone of what Hermeticists called the doctrine of correspondences—the material world was the lesser reflection of the superior spiritual world. The phrase would appear in numerous places in occult writings among authors who had no familiarity with the Hermetic literature. However, that literature is interesting in itself in spelling out a variation on the Gnostic myth. In the *Poimandres*, the most substantive of the Hermetic texts, for example, Hermes is visited in a dream by Poimandres, who describes himself as the "Mind of the Sovereignty." Poimandres relates, by word and picture, the story of the emanation (or creation) of the world from God. "Life is the union of word and mind," he said. First there was Mind also seen as Light. The Word came from the Light, the son of God. The Light also consisted of numerous Powers that constituted an ordered yet unbounded world, the archetypal form that existed before all things and all time.

In his vision there appeared a darkness that transformed into a watery substance. This substance received the Word and in the receiving was thus fashioned into an orderly world. The elements (earth, air, fire, and water) separated. The first Mind, which is bisexual in nature, then made a second Mind, a maker of things. Out of fire and air, the second Mind made seven Administrators (the seven planets known to the ancient world), who oversaw destiny (an allusion to astrology). The Word, being of like substance to Mind the Maker, then united with it to create the world of living creatures—bird, fish, beast.

At this point the first Mind stepped into the process to give birth to Human, a being like unto itself (who was, among other characteristics, bisexual). Taking delight in Human, God gave all the world to it. The first Mind turned over the world shaped by Mind the Maker to Human. Human chose to live in this world of "matter devoid of reason." Human is thus unique, being immortal by origin and as a result having all things within Its Power, but sharing in mortality and thus subject to destiny, desire, and oblivion.

Human created seven entities like unto Itself, also bisexual. After a period the bodies that bound the entities in their bisexual natures were loosed, and all creatures were separated as male and female. These new beings were told to multiply and let all humans recognize that they are immortal and that the cause of death is carnal desire. Those who recognize their immortality return to God; those trapped in carnal desire wander the darkness

183

of the sense world, suffering repeated deaths. However, those who in this world receive the gnosis can escape and return.

The Kabbalah and Hermeticism represent the culmination of medieval Gnostic speculation. The depth of thought that stands behind both is witnessed by their continued ability to inspire people, by way of modern Gnosticism, in the twentieth century. How modern Gnosticism led to the founding of the New Age movement and ultimately to the establishment of Ramtha's School of Enlightenment is discussed more fully in chapter 3.

184

NOTES

CHAPTER 1

1. Unless otherwise stated, material for this chapter was drawn from JZ's autobiography, *A State of Mind: My Story*, and from several interviews with her.

2. The Book of Judith is found in the Apocrypha, that section of Hebrew writings not found in the Protestant editions of the Bible but included by Roman Catholics in the scriptural canon.

3. Douglas Dean, et al., *Executive ESP*.

4. Max Toth and Gary Nielsen, *Pyramid Power*.

CHAPTER 2

1. The idea of the lost continents of Atlantis and Lemuria as the originating point of humanity emerged in the early twentieth century as an alternative to the equally obscure Garden of Eden located in the Tigris-Euphrates Valley in modern-day Iraq. It was originally posited by Helena P. Blavatsky, co-founder of the Theosophical Society, but was developed by Theosophist William Scott-Elliott and culminated in *The Story of Atlantis, and, The Lost Lemuria*. The continent of Atlantis was known from the ancient writings of Plato, who used the story to make several points in his political theory.

The story of Lemuria is an altogether different matter. The idea of the continent began in the nineteenth century when several biologists posited of a land bridge between southern Africa and India as a means of explaining the odd distribution of the lemur. That hypothesis has been replaced with our contemporary understanding of continental drift. However, as picked up by Madame Blavatsky, Lemuria became a Pacific equivalent of Atlantis and an integral element in her understanding of cosmic evolution. From Theosophy the idea passed into the occult community and more recently was accepted by many New Agers. For a more complete discussion, see J. Gordon Melton, Jerome Clark, and Aidan Kelly, eds., *New Age Encyclopedia*.

2. *Ramtha*, ed. Steven L. Weinberg, 7. This book and Deborah Kerins, *The Spinner of Tales*, provided the information about Ramtha. *The Spinner of Tales* is a collection of Ramtha stories.

3. See chapter 7 for a discussion of ascension.

4. Kerins, *The Spinner of Tales*, 60–66, 18–20.

5. Ibid., 87. Listening to Ramtha was not as difficult as later reading what he had said. However, most are happy that in recent years he has learned to speak more normally.

6. Knight, *A State of Mind*, 312, 324. Ramtha did not open JZ's eyes for some time, and when it finally occurred, Jeremy was quite unprepared.

7. On fake mediumship, see J. Gordon Melton, *Encyclopedia of Occultism and Parapsychology*.

8. After several decades of concentrated study, the first generation of parapsychologists were distinctly disinterested. However, in the last few decades the issue has been renewed by psychological discussions of the spectrum of dissociative states of consciousness. These range from pathological states, such as multiple personality disorder, to functional states, such as self-induced trance states seen in mediumship. Contemporary studies have also developed a multicultural aspect because such states have different evaluations in different cultural settings. Psychological studies have concentrated more on mapping the subconscious, especially by using the monitoring equipment now available, than in attempting to verify the objective nature of a possessing entity that manifests in spirit-possession cases. For an introduction to contemporary studies, see Robert Ornstein, *Multimind*; L. Tinnin, "Mental Unity, Altered States of Consciousness, and Dissociation," *Dissociation* 3 (1990): 154–59; and Steven Jay Lynn and Judith W. Rhue, eds., *Dissociation: Clinical and Theoretical Perspectives*.

9. Elizabeth A. Sharp, *William Sharp (Fiona Macleod): A Memoir*, 424. Among Sharp's books originally published under the name Fiona Macleod are *The Divine Adventure*, *The Immortal Hour*, and *The Sin-Eater*.

10. Compare Walter Franklin Prince, *The Case of Patience Worth*; and Irving Litvag, *Singer in the Shadows: The Strange Case of Patience Worth*.

CHAPTER 3

1. On the modern Gnostic tradition, see Antoine Faivre and Jacob Needleman, eds., *Modern Esoteric Spirituality*; Peter Washington, *Madame Blavatsky's Baboon: A History of the Mystics, Mediums, and Misfits Who Brought Spiritualism to America*; Joscelyn Godwin, *The Theosophical Enlightenment*; and "Ancient Wisdom Family," in J. Gordon Melton, *Encyclopedia of American Religions*.

2. A most helpful introduction to Rosicrucianism, and the reference used for this section, is provided by Christopher McIntosh, *The Rosy Cross Unveiled*. The basic texts are most accessible in Paul M. Allen, comp., *A Christian Rosenkreutz Anthology*. For a recent edition with scholarly introduction and notes, see Valentin Andrae [Christian Rosencreutz, pseud.], *Fama Fraternitatis* (1614); *Confessio Fraternitatis* (1615); *Chymische Hochzeit: Christiani Rosencreutz, Anno 1459* (1616), ed. Richard van Dülmen.

3. The lands he traveled spread across the Islamic world. That world had, only a few centuries before, become the source of vast new information released into Europe, not the least of which were the lost writings of Aristotle. In the form of the Ottoman Empire, it was also then engaged in a two-century-old struggle with the Christian world. It had taken Constantinople in 1453 and had made its way to the gates of Vienna early in the next century. By the time Andrae emerged, the Christian world was on the offensive, but it would be many years before the Ottomans were pushed out of the Balkans.

4. Julius F. Sachse, *The German Pietists of Provincial Pennsylvania, 1694–1708*.

5. There is a vast literature on Masonry, including a large body of anti-Masonic writings that has attacked the organizations for their secrecy and perceived anti-Christian teachings. On the history and growth of modern speculative Masonry, see Roy A. Wells, *The Rise and Development of Organized Freemasonry*; Allen E. Roberts, *Freemasonry in American History*; Mary Ann Clawson, *Constructing Brotherhood: Class, Gender, and Fraternalism*; and Richard William Weisberger, *Speculative Freemasonry and the Enlightenment*. For more discussion on Masonic theology, see Albert Pike, *Morals and Dogma of the Ancient and Accepted Scottish Rite of Freemasonry*; and J. D. Buck, *Mystic Masonry*.

6. See the appendix for information on the Kabbalists.

7. The warfare between Masonry and the Catholic Church has had far-reaching implications and has spilled over into other controversies. An illustrative incident was traced by Massimo Introvigne, "The Devil-Makers: Contemporary Evangelical Anti-Mormonism," *Dialogue: A Journal of Mormon Thought* 27, no. 1 (spring 1994): 153–69.

8. On Randolph, see John Patrick Deveney, *Paschal Beverly Randolph: A Nineteenth-Century Black American Spiritualist, Rosicrucian, and Sex Magician*, and shorter treatments in Joscelyn Godwin, *The Theosophical Enlightenment*; and J. Gordon Melton, "Paschal Beverly Randolph: America's Pioneer Occultist," in Jean-Baptiste Martin and Francoise LaPlantine, ed., *Le Defi Magique: Esoterisme, Occultisme, Spiritisme*.

9. For an overview of twentieth-century Rosicrucian groups, see Melton, *Encyclopedia of American Religions*.

10. A handy presentation prepared by Emogene S. Simmons is the two-volume *Introductory Study Course in Theosophy*. Its basic teachings are also in such books as Charles W. Leadbeater, *A Textbook of Theosophy*; and Theosophical Society, *A Primer of Theosophy: A Very Condensed Outline*. On the Masters' modern appearances, see Curuppumullage Jinarajadasa, *The Early Teachings of the Masters, 1881–1883*, and *Letters from the Masters of Wisdom*; Charles W. Leadbeater, *The Masters and the Path*; Lynn F. Perkins, *The Masters As New Age Mentors*; and Elizabeth Clare Prophet, *The Great White Brotherhood in the History, Culture, and Religion of America*. Most New Age channelers have claimed to be in contact with at least one Master of the Great White Brotherhood; many UFO contactees have claimed that what were earlier thought of as Masters were in fact members of a government operating throughout the galaxy.

CHAPTER 4

1. Knight, *A State of Mind*, 377.

2. Prosperity consciousness relates not so much to metaphysical laws as to social realities in an open and fairly wealthy society. The possibilities of significant upward economic mobility depend upon the level of openness as well as the presence of significant amounts of excess wealth. In contemporary America it is also dependent upon an understanding that our society does not as a whole reward hard work so much as the ability to organize and manipulate social resources. Thus, a person who understands how to work with a staff and use its specialized skills (i.e., a manager) will be paid more than the skillful artisan who knows how to

produce the company's product. Protestants, because of their ties to capitalism, have had a more positive approach to wealth than have Roman Catholics but have viewed as problematic the idea of uniting wealth with piety or sanctity and have reacted against attempts to place wealth in the hands of spiritual leaders. It is perfectly permissible for pastors to have incomes slightly below the medians of their congregations, but those who manifest significant attempts to better themselves financially are heavily criticized. Pastors remain the lowest paid of our highly trained professions. The Catholic perspective, which values the vow of poverty by members of religious orders, and the Protestant, which sees the integrity of religious leaders to be at least partially based upon their nonparticipation in the larger economic order, provide a context for the critique of religious leaders who deviate from these norms. Recently, the simple denunciation of his display of wealth was integral to turning public opinion against television preacher Jim Bakker at a time when most of his former supporters simply did not understand the legal technicalities that led to his downfall. Everyone understood that Bakker was, by the standards of the average viewer, drawing an exorbitant salary. On prosperity consciousness, see Catherine Ponder, *The Dynamic Laws of Prosperity*; Sanaya Roman and Duane Packer, *Creating Money*; and Charles Fillmore, *Prosperity*.

The issue of money has split the New Age community. Those New Agers most attuned to ecology and other social concerns have been very active in arguing that only limited resources exist and that the transformation (i.e., destruction) of long-term resources into ephemeral wealth must stop. They advocate simple living at a below-average economic level and a focus upon the enjoyment of life in ways that do not "steal" from others who may be less wise or less strong in the ways of acquiring a share of the world's good.

3. Fawn Vrazo, "Indeed!" *Albuquerque Journal Magazine* (May 31, 1983): 12, 14–15.

4. The term *religion* has Christian roots, *religion* and *Christianity* at one point being synonymous. As comparative religion developed, other religions were compared to the similarity of belief and function as Christianity. Many laws, now definitely archaic, were based upon this kind of consideration and for legal purposes defined religion in terms of relationship to a theistic God and the worship of him, a matter of considerable difficulty to nontheistic religions such as Humanism and Theravada Buddhism.

5. For an overview of the New Age movement, see Paul Heelas, *The New Age Movement*; Richard Kyle, *The New Age Movement in American Culture*; and William Bloom, ed., *The New Age: An Anthology of Essential Writings*.

6. Jess Stern, *Soul Mates*, 129.

7. Shirley MacLaine, *Dancing in the Light*, 125–27, 135; Stern, *Soul Mates*, 119.

8. Robin Westen, *Channelers: A New Age Directory*, 109.

9. See John Ballou Newbrough, *Oahspe: A New Bible in the Words of Jehovih and His Angel Embassadors . . .* ; and Levi H. Dowling, *The Aquarian Gospel of Jesus the Christ*. For a historical and bibliographical survey of the extensive channeling literature, see Joel Bjorling, *Channeling: A Bibliographic Exploration*.

10. On Cayce's channeling activity, see Harmon Hartzell Bro, *A Seer Out of Season: The Life of Edgar Cayce*; and Thomas Segrue, *There Is a River: The Story of Edgar Cayce*. In addition, the Association for Research and Enlightenment in Virginia Beach, Virginia, has published many examples of Cayce's channeled material. On Bailey, see John R. Sinclair, *The Alice Bailey Inheritance*. The Arcane School keeps the Alice A. Bailey channeled material in print, among the more important being *Discipleship in the New Age*, *A Treatise on Cosmic Fire*, and *A Treatise on White Magic*. Ballard's most important work as a messenger was published as the third volume of the Saint Germain series from the I AM Religious Activity. His channeled messages were then published as articles in the *I AM Voice* and later reprinted as additional volumes in the Saint Germain Series. See Great Cosmic Being Mighty Victory, *The "I AM" Discourses*.

11. J. Gordon Melton and George M. Eberhart, *The Flying Saucer Contactee Movement: 1950–1990*.

12. In the wake of the channeling fad in the 1980s, several books appeared, including William H. Kautz and Melanie Brannon, *Channeling: The Intuitive Connection*; Jon Klimo, *Channeling: Investigations on Receiving Information from Paranormal Sources*; Joe Fisher, *Hungry Ghosts: An Investigation into Channeling and the Spirit World*; and Arthur Hastings, *With the Tongues of Men and Angels: A Study of Channeling*. Of these, the Hastings volume is the most reliable.

13. *Ramtha*, ed. Weinberg, 2.

14. A discussion of the changes is found in *Ramtha: An Introduction*, ed. Weinberg, 45–47. Many physiological changes were monitored in the psychological tests discussed in chapter 8.

15. Ramtha, *Love Yourself into Life*, ed. Weinberg, ix.

16. This is a point to which we will return in chapter 8 when we discuss critics of JZ and Ramtha. A helpful beginning is in "Nothing But Truth," chapter 12 in *Ramtha*, ed. Weinberg.

17. *Love Yourself into Life*, ed. Weinberg, 146–47.

18. *Ramtha: An Introduction*, ed. Weinberg, 64; *Ramtha*, ed. Weinberg, 35.

19. *Ramtha*, ed. Weinberg, 29–30, 20–21. The Unknown God is a reference from the Apostle Paul's sermon on the Areopagus in Acts 17:16–31.

20. Among the most popular analyses of world-shaping philosophy appeared in the writings of Thomas Troward in the early twentieth century. Troward built his philosophy on the insights of the new psychology, especially the exciting discoveries about the mind revealed in the phenomenon of hypnosis, from which he developed the idea of the objective and subjective mind. The objective mind was roughly equivalent to the normal waking consciousness. The subjective mind was equated with the subconscious, especially that aspect of the mind revealed through the hypnotic trance.

The subjective mind seemed awesome in many ways. It could implement suggestions given to it far beyond the ability of the objective mind to do so. The subjective mind, Troward suggested, reasons deductively. It can draw the necessary conclusions from looking at two propositions presented to it. It operates on the truthfulness of assumptions that have been given to it throughout life. It takes the thoughts imposed upon it by the objective mind and deductively works out their final consequences. The body receives the effects of the subjective mind's activity. The subjective mind builds the body according to the suggestions fed to it by the objective mind.

Troward reasoned that the state of one's body was conditioned by the beliefs of one's subjective mind. He then extended his observations to the individual's conditions in life. People tended to have around them what their subconscious minds have been told they should have. If they wanted to improve their lives, their objective minds must impress the new conditions upon their subconscious minds and allow their subconscious minds step-by-step to re-create the immediate environment. Troward's thoughts became the basis of Ernest Holmes's teachings, upon which the Church of Religious Science was founded.

For additional information, see Thomas Troward, *The Edinburgh Lectures on Mental Science*. See also Ernest Holmes, *The Science of Mind*.

21. *Ramtha*, ed. Weinberg, 101.

22. Ibid., 144.

23. I have made no attempt to verify the elements in JZ's autobiography. Several reporters who wrote feature articles on JZ and Ramtha noted their attempts and only uncovered, as was to be expected, different

perspectives on the events but no discrepancies that would suggest JZ was consciously falsifying her past. I did speak with her son Chris who retold some of the incidents from his perspective. He missed some details but added others. Not an active member of Ramtha's school, he has some different observations about his mother but no doubts about her sincerity. Although he experienced some incidents very differently, he found no errors in her reporting. Such is to be expected. We all experience the same events differently and invest them with varying degrees of significance.

24. Khit Harding, *Becoming: A Master's Manual*; Ramtha, *Love Yourself into Life*, ed. Weinberg; and Schuler Ingle, "Here's Ramtha!" *New Age Journal*, June 1986, 12.

25. "JZ Knight/Ramtha in Sydney, 7/8th November 1987," *Australia's New Age News* 1, no. 10 (December 1987): 1, 20.

26. A transcript of this constituting event was published as Ramtha, *The Ancient Schools of Wisdom*, comp. Diane Munoz-Smith.

CHAPTER 5

1. *Ramtha*, ed. Weinberg, 7. As of the beginning of 1996, Ramtha's philosophical teachings had not been committed to print. During my research and writing, they were available only orally in class or on audiotapes made at each session. They have also undergone constant development as Ramtha introduces new metaphors to explain his worldview and the new spiritual practices he gives to advanced students. Of the written texts (transcripts of Ramtha's speeches), only the White Book (the common name for *Ramtha*) and *The Ancient Schools of Wisdom*, comp. Munoz-Smith, laid out his philosophical system. However, early in 1996 a variety of tapes was released to the public, and work has begun on editing and publishing them in both audio and print. *A Beginner's Guide to Creating Reality* (JZK Publishing), one set of instructions from a beginning weekend event, is scheduled for release in 1997.

2. *Ramtha*, ed. Weinberg, 48–49.

3. Students of Christian history will connect with those forms of Christian theology heavily influenced by Platonic philosophy and most closely to the mystical *via negativa* of Christian mysticism. However, in spite of the connections that could be made with the more abstract levels of Christian theology, the distinction between Ramtha's perspective and Christianity is important. The affirmation of God as the Almighty One who created the world through an act of will leads naturally to worship as the proper response. God as the Void calls for no

such worshipful response. The individual's relationship to the variant understanding of deity is, therefore, completely different, starting from the beginning of creation.

4. Students have a basic problem understanding one point in Gnosticism. The emanation of the world from the indescribable beginning point is done with spatial metaphors. However, these metaphors veil a more basic nonspatial psychological understanding of the self as embodying all the levels in the self. To understand the limited reality of the spatial metaphor, one must experience the psychological reality of what the spatial metaphor is attempting to express. That experience is given through the school's spiritual disciplines.

5. For example, see near-death experiences recounted in such books as Raymond Moody's *Life After Life* and its sequels. On this point, however, Ramtha separates himself from most New Age teachings. For him, the third level, the level of light, is relatively low in the vast scheme of things and in relation to the seventh level. But it is this realm about which most New Agers write and toward which they direct readers and students. It is also, according to Ramtha, the realm of the Christian heaven. The Christian God dwells there. The Christian God is light. The Christian God is also male, and above the third level in Ramtha's system there is no gender differentiation.

6. In discussing the lower realms, the light and astral worlds, the teachings clearly connect with nineteenth- and twentieth-century metaphysical movements such as Spiritualism and Theosophy. Ramtha notes the mapping of these worlds under a variety of names. His primary difference from the more traditional presentation of these realms concerns the nature of one's interaction with them.

7. In the creation and evolution of the human body, Ramtha draws on references to the biblical creation story in the opening chapters of the book of Genesis. He interprets the Genesis story as a somewhat distorted account of the actual process. God (i.e., the gods) shaped Adam (the human body) out of the clay of the earth (the particles of energy and matter). The gods shaped man in their own image (i.e., they "imaged" a body based upon the light and astral bodies as they then existed). In making reference to the Genesis story, Ramtha connects his creation myth to a more familiar myth; however, he reinterprets the myth in such a way as to remove much of the male bias. Existence above the third level is genderless, and the two genders are created simultaneously. This is especially significant to many female students. Here Ramtha uses *dream* to mean holding in consciousness and energized thought.

8. Genesis 2:21–22.

9. J. B. Phillips, *Ring of Truth*, 118–19. See Karlis Osis and Eriendur Haraldsson, *At the Hour of Death*, for a variety of accounts of the experience of death, including sightings of the astral body.

10. I discovered how common both astral plane and light plane experiences were when as a pastor I let my parishioners know that I was interested in their experiences as Christians and asked them to share with me things that had happened that confirmed their faith. As they saw that I listened and commented but without denigrating or ridiculing, they shared innumerable stories of seeing apparitions of their recently deceased relatives and of receiving inner guidance, answers to prayers, and visions of angels.

11. Nineteenth-century Spiritualism emerged as a popular religious movement offering people access to the surviving spirits on what Ramtha would call the astral realm and began to delineate what were considered rather inaccessible levels beyond. It also taught means through clairvoyance and telepathy by which people could access the psychic realm and held psychic development classes to that end. The spirits also promoted the practice of spiritual healing. Psychical research has studied these groups in hopes that they were on to something. Traditional religious groups of all kinds have recognized the validity of spirit contacts and have valued and made a place for such contacts. They also have used sacred and supernatural language (miracles, gifts of the Holy Spirit, etc.) to describe contacts. However, religious people tend to view these events as haphazard, arbitrary (occurring only as God decides to act), or in the domain of unique people (saints and mystics). They shy away from any attempt to transform these extraordinary experiences into everyday events, because if miracles began to happen to everyone every day, they would cease to be miracles. That difference in approach to spiritual experiences creates a major distinction in lifestyles between those in metaphysical traditions and those who adhere to more traditional faiths, especially Western theism.

In this light one can see the peculiar space in the religious world created by Pentecostalism. Pentecostal churches are perfectly orthodox in overall belief and practice. They also place a great emphasis upon each member's active life with the Holy Spirit. As a sign of the indwelling of the Spirit, members are expected to speak in tongues. As a continued sign of the Spirit's presence, members manifest various gifts of the Spirit, such as the word of wisdom (which to an outside observer looks very much like telepathy and clairvoyance), prophecy (which resembles precognition), and divine healing (which resembles psychic healing). Great value is placed upon exercising these gifts during worship services and other less formal gatherings. Revivals are said to occur when a rich manifestation of the gifts erupts in a particular time and place. Ministers (such as Oral Roberts) who have regularly demonstrated such gifts are assigned the highest status. On the other extreme, ministers unable to demonstrate such gifts regularly have attempted to gain their status by adopting the same mentalist tricks previously used by fake Spiritualist mediums in order to make it appear that such gifts are operating in their ministry.

12. In describing "primitive" humans, Ramtha has an occasion to introduce a theme that is an undercurrent in the teachings and becomes important at the higher levels. *Homo erectus* was not beautiful by contemporary standards, but beauty is to be understood as relative, relative to the dictates of a degenerate society. By primitive humans' standards, they were beautiful. In many areas Ramtha's students will have experiences and develop patterns that may set them apart from the norm. They may be viewed as engaged in weird ideas and practices. However, as they shift their perspectives, they will also learn that certain outward appearances are unimportant. This idea also appears in many forms in many faiths.

195

CHAPTER 6

1. For a more traditional understanding of the chakras, see Charles W. Leadbeater, *The Chakras*; Anodea Judith, *Wheels of Life: A User's Guide to the Chakra System*; Zachery F. Landsdowne, *The Chakras and Esoteric Healing*; and Peter Rendel, *Introduction to the Chakras*. Although the existence of ten chakras is mentioned in the more technical literature (shown in different locations depending upon whether the body is pictured sitting or standing), commonly only seven are discussed and used in theosophical teachings.

2. The idea of kundalini was introduced into the West in the late nineteenth century and was publicized in books published by the Theosophical Society. In "The Hindu System of Medicine," a prize essay by B. D. Basu published in *Guy's Hospital Gazette* (London, 1889), an early attempt was made to relate the tantric understanding of the body and the chakra system with the human nervous system. In traditional teachings the kundalini is aroused in one of two ways. The yogi may engage in a combination of hatha yoga posturing (*asanas*), breathing (*pranayama*), and various combinations of concentration and meditation. Or the devotee may approach a guru (teacher) who will, through

a process called *shaktipat*, stimulate the kundalini psychically, thus arousing it. Ramtha does not teach *asanas*, and he specifically eschews meditation in favor of concentration.

One American teacher, Pierre Bernard (1875–1955), also known to his followers as Oom the Magnificent, taught a form of kundalini yoga through the first half of the twentieth century at his ashram on Long Island. However, it was not until the late 1960s that gurus who taught kundalini yoga began to popularize the idea in North America. Possibly the first was Yogi Bhajan, leader of the Sikh Dharma. He was followed by a host of gurus such as Yogi Desai, Swami Muktananda, and Pandit Gopi Krishna. Gopi Krishna tried to go beyond Basu in arguing for a biological basis for kundalini. See Gopi Krishna, *The Biological Basis of Religion and Genius*.

3. What is summarized in the ensuing text is taught in a step-by-step manner with precise instructions. Because this volume is not meant as a C&E manual, I have concentrated on presenting the overall practice and on analyzing its intent.

4. There is a vast literature on Kirlian photography, but a final summary and list of relevant research is in Henri E. Montandon, "Psychophysiological Aspects of the Kirlian Phenomenon: A Confirmatory Study," *Journal of the American Society for Psychical Research* 71, no. 1 (January 1977): 45–49.

5. At this point, Ramtha is relating his understanding of the energy field around the body to the electromagnetic spectrum, the various forms taken by radiant energy as it passes through space and time. In order of decreasing energy, the principle forms of radiation are termed *gamma rays, X rays, ultraviolet, visible light, infrared, micro,* and *radio*. Max Plank introduced the idea that radiant energy is best understood as being emitted in discrete amounts, i.e., *quanta*, and Einstein suggested that the quanta were best understood as particles which he termed *photon*. The energy of each photon is directly related to the frequency of the associated radiation.

6. This practice as observed in Tibet was described by Alexandria David-Neel in *Magic and Mystery in Tibet*.

7. This idea was dramatically presented in the *Star Trek* episode called "Wink of an Eye" in which Captain Kirk and the crew of the *Enterprise* visit a planet from which they had received a distress call, only to find it uninhabited. In trying to figure out the problem, Kirk drank coffee made from the local water. He seemed to disappear, but in fact his metabolic rate had increased to match that of the planet's inhabitants. They were moving (vibrating) so fast that they were invisible to the slow-moving

crew. They could see the ship's crew, but the crew could not see the inhabitants even though they occupied the same space. Attempts to verbally communicate with the crew were heard only as a buzzing noise, like playing a record at the wrong speed. Eventually Kirk was able to write a note and leave it for the crew, who found it, solved the problem, and retrieved the valiant captain.

8. See, for example, the testimonies on Ramtha's audiotape *The Emotional Body*, September 5, 1994, Ramtha Dialogues. Although I make no scientific claims for the reported healings (they are too new and as yet not independently documented), they are nevertheless interesting and exciting stories, as are all accounts of people who have been healed by their attention to the spiritual realm. I must admit to being duly impressed when I saw the new, half-grown upper front teeth of one woman who had graciously interrupted her evening to meet with me.

CHAPTER 7

1. One popular writer for *The Golden Thread*, Kathy Arnold, has published *Manifestations of Greatness*, a compilation of her columns built around the experiences of Ramtha.

2. J. Gordon Melton and Robert L. Moore, *The Cult Experience: Responding to the New Religious Pluralism*. On the stages of life, see Daniel J. Levison, *The Seasons of a Man's Life*, or the popular books that have built on his insights.

3. The midlife crisis was first recognized as a phenomenon in the 1960s and became more generally recognized in the 1970s. The term refers to successful executives who became frustrated with their careers and suddenly, often without warning to friends and colleagues, quit their jobs and sought employment in totally unrelated fields; often they became self-employed. Others went through traumatic divorces and began living out what their friends saw as strong fantasies, suddenly completely altering their social lives. Women frequently go through that transition as part of their adjustment to their youngest children leaving home. Among Ramtha's advanced students, women outnumber men 3 to 1.

4. Constance Jones, "Students in Ramtha's School of Enlightenment: A Profile from Demographic Survey, Narrative, and Interview," a paper presented at the conference "In Search of the Self," Yelm, Washington, February 8–9, 1997 (forthcoming).

5. Some of Ramtha's comments on UFOs were published in *UFOs and the Nature of Reality*, ed. Judi Pope Koteen.

6. See also Frank Don, *Earth Changes Ahead*; and Hugh Lynn Cayce, *Earth Changes Update*.

7. *I Am Ramtha*, ed. Cindy Black, Richard Cohn, and Greg Simmons, 76–77. In my own survey of the New Age, the most horrendous predictions concerning Earth changes came from author and channeler Ruth Montgomery, who has predicted a polar shift in 1999 that will usher in the New Age by killing the majority of Earth's residents. See Ruth Montgomery, *Aliens Among Us*. It is these more dire apocalyptic pronouncements to which Ramtha seems to be responding.

8. *Ramtha Intensive: Change, the Days to Come*, ed. Steven L. Weinberg, Carol Wright, and John Clancy. As a resident of Santa Barbara, California, I thought it seemingly more than coincidence that my research on this book began not long after a major fire in Santa Barbara had consumed almost 500 homes and had come within two blocks of my office; and events in nearby Los Angeles included a major earthquake, and devastating fires and flooding that destroyed a part of Malibu. While I was working on this chapter in January 1995, a major earthquake centered in Kobe, Japan, filled the news, coincidentally on the first anniversary of the Los Angeles quake. Simultaneously, the state of California and Santa Barbara in particular had major flooding because of two weeks of continuous rain. JZ quietly reminded me of these events as substantiation of Ramtha's words.

9. Typical was the situation of actress Linda Evans. In excruciating detail she told of the breakup of her marriage to John Derek and in the midst of her attempts to pick up the pieces became part of the New Age milieu. Evans had based a good deal of her self-image on her relationship with her husband, and, as she later put it, "I wanted to find something within me that was okay without a man." After a decade of searching and discovering little more than salves to temporarily dull the ache, in 1985 she discovered Ramtha, and eventually she and JZ became friends. In the late 1980s she purchased a home near Tacoma and eventually pulled up roots in Beverly Hills and relocated to Washington full time as an active student. See Jean-Noel Bassior, "Talking with Linda Evans: A Psychic Changed My Life," *Redbook*, May 1988, 86–88.

Some of the concern about students moving to Washington was fueled by the contemporaneous events surrounding the attempt to build Rajneeshpuram, a city for the followers of the Indian spiritual teacher Rajneesh (Osho), and the development of a community of members of the Church Universal and Triumphant in a valley directly north of Yellowstone Park in Montana. Most of the concern centered upon antidevelopment interests in several communities who wished to stop the flow of people into what they saw as a stable rural area.

10. Though highly atypical, in 1990 several students started to construct underground bunkers, a project abandoned after it was discovered and publicized in the press.

11. My informal observations were confirmed in the community study made by Charles LeWarne in 1996, "The Pride of the Prairie Encounters Ramtha," presented at the conference "In Search of the Self," Yelm, Washington, February 8–9, 1997. He noted that the fears and anger expressed during the early years of the school have been allayed. He added, "The Ramtha students have achieved a degree of acceptance in various aspects of community life even as they have had an effect in altering it" (forthcoming).

12. Ramtha's understanding of the One World Order is in the opening sections of *Last Waltz of the Tyrants*, ed. Judi Pope Koteen. Often associated with the Rothschild conspiracy theory is a virulent anti-Semitism and, in the late twentieth century, political opposition to the United Nations. It is to Ramtha's credit that neither element is present.

13. Klimo, *Channeling: Investigations on Receiving Information from Paranormal Sources.*

14. Regarding former student charges, see Leslie Brown, "Ramtha's New Age Shrouded in Doom," *The Morning News Tribune*, May 24, 1992. There was some basis for the charges. First, for example, there are certainly people at the school who are competing for JZ's attention. That is almost a given. It has occurred ever since JZ attained her celebrity status and will, unfortunately, continue for the rest of her life. In comparison with leaders of other new religions I have studied, Knight/Ramtha have done little to encourage such competition, and I find the small element of truth in the charge little reason to criticize either JZ or the school. Second, the school has developed as a mystery school, and inherent in such a school is a heightened degree of secrecy not present in the early and mid-1980s. Such secrecy also requires some obedience at least as regards not discussing with outsiders the inner workings of the school. One can certainly hold the opinion, and it is one with which I have great sympathy, that spiritual matters should not be a matter of secrecy, that all the teachings should be available at any time to any seeker. But again, that is a matter about which sincere and devout spiritually minded people disagree, and there are good arguments on both sides. One can, additionally, understand a certain bitterness felt by someone who believed that the group had moved from an open to a more closed position.

During and immediately after the 1992 trial, the proceedings of which were front page news for several weeks, JZ, as may be expected, was somewhat angry at having to go through the public ordeal with her ex-husband. I found that students were concerned about the proceedings, but, although a few haunted the courtroom, most were fairly blasé. They read the papers and watched the news on television and were mildly upset that the image being portrayed in the media did not conform to their experience of the school. A few expressed hurt at being shunned or spoken ill of by neighbors simply because they attend the school, but they seemed to have learned to take such behavior in stride.

15. The term *ascension* was used prominently by Guy W. Ballard, founder of the I AM movement in the 1930s, and from it and from a related I AM group (the Church Universal and Triumphant) the idea passed into and became popular in the New Age movement. Ascension is a Christian theme that has a certain appeal to Gnostic groups who would reject the idea of resurrection of the body in any orthodox Christian sense. For example, every summer the I AM movement presents a pageant on the life of Jesus at Mt. Shasta, California. The story line of the pageant moves, in accord with I AM teachings, from the Lord's Supper directly to the ascension, skipping entirely any mention of the crucifixion. On the contemporary New Age use of ascension, see Joshua David Stone, *The Complete Ascension Manual for the Aquarian Age*; Joanna Cherry, *Ascension for You and Me*; and Tony Stubbs, *An Ascension Handbook*.

16. *Ramtha*, ed. Weinberg, 71.

CHAPTER 8

1. It appears that, putting aside all his critical skills and ignoring the consistent reports of those who had actually investigated the reports, Raschke accepted at face value the testimonies of a variety of people concerning the reality of Satanism in America. Throughout the 1980s several law enforcement officials as well as scholars had gone looking for the Satanists and had come up over and over again with stories that dissolved under outside scrutiny. Most recently, two federally funded researchers, Philip Shaver of the University of California at Davis and Pamala Freyed of the False Memory Syndrome Foundation, conducted a nationwide survey and, after examining 12,000 cases, could find none with any factual base.

2. Katherine Lowry, "Channelers," *Omni* 10 (March 1988): 46–50, 146–50.

3. Texe Marrs, *Dark Secrets of the New Age*, 95–96, and *Mystery Mark of the New Age*, 117.

4. Lowry, "Channelers," *Omni*, 146.

5. Klimo, *Channeling: Investigations on Receiving Information from Paranormal Sources*, 342.

6. Ibid., 44. This was a perspective voiced repeatedly by Steven Bakker, the former Ramtha staff member who appeared on *20/20*. See also Allen Spraggett, *Arthur Ford, the Man Who Talked with the Dead*.

7. The story of JZ's meeting and marriage to Jeff Knight is discussed in some detail in her autobiography, *A State of Mind*. She and Jeff shared an interest in things spiritual and a passion for Arabian horses. At one point she believed him to be her soul mate. Many people in the Spiritualist movements and other psychic groups have posited the existence of a person to whom one somehow (explanations vary) has a cosmic relationship. The sign of one's soul mate is usually a mixture of intense passion with an experience of communion on a more spiritual level. (Ramtha was introduced to many people in Jess Stern's *Soul Mates* on the subject.) Unfortunately, after a passionate relationship, Jeff's bisexuality asserted itself and he began to develop new relationships in the gay community, the knowledge of which he kept from JZ. He also developed AIDS and even after he knew he was ill exposed her to infection. They were divorced in 1989. At the time of their separation, he received the cash reserves and moved from the ranch while she assumed all the debts from the failure of the Arabian horse business, which had reached into seven figures. The last years of Jeff Knight's life (he died in 1994) were spent in contesting the divorce settlement in light of JZ's subsequent financial recovery, though his efforts were denied by the courts.

8. Ken Harrell, "Psychic Ordered Linda Evans to Rub Her Face in Horse Dung—And She Did," *Globe*, July 14, 1992, 19.

9. With few exceptions, even the charges of insincerity from the leaders have nothing to do with the groups or the leaders. They are simply statements by nonbelievers that they find the religion unbelievable. As is often the case, religious myths often include unconventional affirmations that, especially when taken out of context, sound irrational, odd, silly, or in direct contradiction to common sense. In the 1940s the state's attorney in Los Angeles took the leaders of the flamboyant I AM Religious Activity to trial on just this argument. The ideas of the I AM were so ridiculous, he argued, that no one could believe them. Therefore, Guy and Edna Ballard must be insincere leaders perpetrating a fraud against the public. That case elicited the famous opinion from

Supreme Court Justice Douglas: that you could not put a person's religious faith, no matter how odd it seems to us at the moment, on trial. People who have ever tried to explain why they believe that a thirty-year-old untutored carpenter who was killed as a criminal several thousand years ago is actually the key to meaning in the universe clearly understand how people not raised in a Christian environment can honestly think, and make laws based on that thinking, that the only way Christian missionaries make converts is by offering them monetary rewards.

10. Jean-Noel Bassior, "Linda Evans and JZ Knight," *Body, Mind and Spirit* 50 (May/June 1992): 45.

11. JZ offered to repay all the investors. Many accepted. Others, some still active in the school, refused to take any money, noting that they had invested with their eyes open and were knowledgeable about the risk. They felt it was their responsibility, not JZ's, to cover their losses. A smaller group turned down JZ's offer and decided to reorganize to gain something from the investment.

12. Ramtha, *Love Yourself into Life*, ed. Weinberg, 217, 214.

13. The position echoes the Westminster Catechism, which sees the goal of life to serve and *enjoy* God forever.

14. *Beginning C&E Workshop*, October 15, 1994, Ramtha Dialogues, audiotape.

15. Catherine Collins and Douglas Franz, "Let Us Prey," *Modern Maturity* 22 (June 1994): 22; John Crutcher, "Ramtha, the Enlightened One?" parts 1 and 2, *Common Ground* 10 (July 1995): 24–27, 38–39; (August 1995); 21–25, 35.

16. Reported in Stanley Krippner et al., "Channeling Ramtha: Psychological and Phenomenological Data"; and Ian Wickramasekera et al., "On the Psychology of Ramtha's School of Enlightenment," papers delivered at the conference "In Search of the Self," Yelm, Washington, February 8–9, 1997 (forthcoming).

EPILOGUE

1. I caution New Agers that the school is not a nice place, it is not an abode of sweetness and light, and it certainly is not for everyone. It is demanding, its disciplines are intensive, and no one is allowed to rest upon past laurels. It is very different from New Age workshops, and participation will be far different from sitting with the latest channeler. It is a new entity on the metaphysical horizon. You have been warned.

2. This superficial approach varied with the group under consideration. The Mormons and Jehovah's Witnesses, large groups with variations
on a familiar Calvinist theology, tended to be more closely studied, but
few took the time to understand even the basic theological framework of
esoteric and non-Christian groups. I still carry with me the intense inter-
change I had with one colleague who wrote about new religions. He had
written one perfectly awful book, and in a piece I wrote I noted that I
could not recommend it because of its multitudinous errors. He wrote me
an angry letter, the kind I usually ignore, but this one caught me on a rare
slow day, so I responded. I took one chapter of the book and in six single-
spaced pages delineated a variety of factual errors (not to mention the
essential omissions) and then noted that I could do the same with every
chapter, each dealing with one of the new religions.

3. Every time a violation of trust occurs, it becomes that much harder
for the next person who seeks access to a group. Such a violation can occur
when a scholar gains the group's confidence and trust merely to use the
information gained to attack or expose the group in a polemic manner.

APPENDIX 203

1. On the origin and history of Gnosticism, see Kurt Rudolph, *Gnosis:
The Nature and History of Gnosticism*; Charles W. Hedrick and Robert
Hodgson, Jr., eds., *Nag Hammadi, Gnosticism, and Early Christianity*;
Robert M. Grant, *Gnosticism: A Source Book of Heretical Writings from the
Early Christian Period*; and Antoine Faivre, *Access to Western Esotericism*.
Still valuable is the classic study by Hans Jonas, *The Gnostic Religion: The
Message of the Alien God and the Beginnings of Christianity*. Since the
findings at Nag Hammadi, the study of Gnosticism has flourished, and
new books and articles frequently appear. For texts of the Gnostic gospels,
see Edgar Hennecke, ed., *New Testament Apocrypha, vol. I, Gospels and
Related Writings*.

In Paul's epistles, certain teachings, later identified with Gnosticism,
are strongly condemned. In the Epistle to the Colossians, for example,
he warns against being beguiled by the enticing words, philosophy, and
traditions of men, including the "worshipping of angels" (2:18). The
first Johannine epistles exhorts the church to test the spirits (i.e., false
prophets), and the test shall be whether they deny that Jesus has come
in the flesh, a basic Gnostic position. Others have seen the whole of the
first chapter of the Gospel of John as an anti-Gnostic text, taking some
of their key words (such as the Greek *logos* or "word") and turning it

back upon them. Still others have traced the origin of Gnosticism to Simon Magus (Acts 8:9–24).

2. I find the arguments in favor of the Christian origin of Gnosticism most persuasive. Gnosticism seems most likely to have emerged within the church as an expression of the salvation teachings and later took on a life of its own and developed a variety of forms not necessarily reliant upon Christianity. See *Irenaeus of Lyons versus Contemporary Gnosticism*, ed. J. T. Nielsen, which reprints all the relevant Gnostic texts quoted by Irenaeus.

3. The Valentian myth is from *The Gospel of Truth*. See Kendrick Grabel, ed., *The Gospel of Truth*, or Hennecke, ed., *New Testament Apocrypha*.

4. Dualist systems see the world divided into two somewhat equal opposing forces of good-evil or darkness-light, with humanity caught in the front line of the battle. See George Widengren, *Mani and Manichaeism*.

5. Milan Loos, *Dualistic Heresy in the Middle Ages*.

6. Compare Israel Regardie, *The Garden of Pomegranates* and *The Middle Pillar: A Co-relation of the Principle of Analytic Psychology and the Elementary Technique of Magic*.

7. Quoted in Grillot de Givry, trans., *A Pictorial Anthology of Witchcraft, Magic and Alchemy*, 349, 350. On the history of alchemy, see Mircea Eliade, *The Forge and the Crucible*; Antoine Faivre, *The Golden Fleece and Alchemy*; and Allison Coudert, *Alchemy: The Philosopher's Stone*.

8. This famous manuscript by Abraham the Jew (b. 1362) was incorporated in a book by Abraham ben Simeon of Worms (15th century) and has been translated and circulated by S. L. MacGregor Mathers as *The Book of the Sacred Magic of Abra-Melin the Mage* . . . and now exists in several editions.

9. de Givry, 366.

10. There are still a few contemporary exponents of alchemy, and certainly psychotherapist Carl G. Jung examined the alchemical texts for their knowledge of the subconscious. For contemporary speculations, see J. H. Reyner, *The Diary of a Modern Alchemist*; Armand Barbault, *Gold of a Thousand Mornings*; and Frater Albertus, *The Alchemist of the Rocky Mountains*.

11. Hermes Trismegistus, *Thrice-Greatest Hermes*, trans. G. R. S. Mead. For an English translation of the Hermetic texts (including *Poimandres*), see Hermes Trismegistus, *Hermetica: The Ancient Greek and Latin Writings* . . . , trans. Walter Scott. *The Emerald Tablet* had been known previously only from a twelfth-century commentary upon it, and its ancient date is mostly conjectural.

BIBLIOGRAPHY

RAMTHA'S SCHOOL OF ENLIGHTENMENT

Books

Arnold, Kathy. *Manifestations of Greatness*. Yelm, Wash.: K. Arnold, 1996.

Harding, Khit. *Becoming: A Master's Manual*. Eastsound, Wash.: Adams Publishing, 1983.

———. *Manifesting: A Master's Manual*. Eastsound, Wash.: Adams Publishing, 1988.

Kerins, Deborah. *The Spinner of Tales: A Collection of Stories As Told by Ramtha*. Yelm, Wash.: New Horizon Publishing, 1991.

Knight, J. Z. *A State of Mind: My Story*. New York: Warner Books, 1987.

Mahr, Douglas. *Destination Freedom: A Time-Travel Adventure*. 2 vols. Englewood Cliffs, N.J.: Prentice-Hall, 1988–89.

———. *Voyage to the New World*. Friday Harbor, Wash.: Masterworks, 1985.

Michael. *Tales of the Ram*. Yelm, Wash.: UPword Press, 1989.

Ohayon-Budhoo, Claude. *Dancing with My Soul*. Fairfield, Iowa: Sunstar Publishing, 1995.

Ramtha (Spirit), [channeled by] J. Z. Knight. *The Ancient Schools of Wisdom: A Collection of Teachings*. Compiled by Diane Munoz-Smith. Yelm, Wash.: Horus Publishing, 1996.

——. *I Am Ramtha*. Edited by Cindy Black, Richard Cohn, and Greg Simmons. Portland, Ore.: Beyond Words Publishing, 1986.

——. *Last Waltz of the Tyrants*. Edited by Judi Pope Koteen. Hillsboro, Ore.: Beyond Words Publishing, 1989.

——. *Love Yourself into Life*. Edited by Steven L. Weinberg. Eastsound, Wash.: Sovereignty, 1983.

——. *Ramtha* [The White Book]. Edited by Steven L. Weinberg. Eastsound, Wash.: Sovereignty, 1986.

——. *Ramtha: An Introduction*. Edited by Steven L. Weinberg. Eastsound, Wash.: Sovereignty, 1988.

——. *Ramtha Intensive: Change, the Days to Come*. Edited by Steven L. Weinberg, Carol Wright, and John Clancy. Eastsound, Wash.: Sovereignty, 1987.

——. *Ramtha Intensive: Soulmates*. Edited by Steven L. Weinberg et al. Eastsound, Wash: Sovereignty, 1987.

——. *UFOs and the Nature of Reality: Understanding Alien Consciousness and Interdimensional Mind*. Edited by Judi Pope Koteen. Eastsound, Wash.: Indelible Ink Publishing, 1990.

Videotapes (Published by Ramtha Productions)

Audience with Ramtha, 1984.
Change: The Days to Come, 1986.
The Next Step: Super Consciousness, 1986.
The Power to Manifest, 1987.
Ramtha and His Teachings, 1986.

Audiotapes (Published by Ramtha Dialogues)

Advanced C & E Workshop, April 27–28, 1991.
Beginning C & E Workshop, February 3–4, 1990.
Beginning C & E Workshop, February 5–6, 1994.
Beginning C & E Workshop, October 15, 1994.
The Emotional Body, September 5, 1994.
An Evening with Ramtha, February 3, 1989.
Selected Stories, 1989.
Yahweh-Jehovah, 1982.

Bibliography

Articles

Anderson, Rick. "While She Tuned to the Spirit, They Repo'ed Her Rolls." *The Seattle Times*, April 18, 1988.

Bassior, Jean-Noel. "Linda Evans and JZ Knight." *Body, Mind and Spirit* 11, no. 3 (May/June 1992): 44–47.

———. "Talking with Linda Evans: A Psychic Changed My Life." *Redbook*, May 1988, 86–88.

Brown, Leslie. "Ramtha's New Age Shrouded in Doom." [Tacoma, Wash.] *The Morning News Tribune*, May 24, 1992.

Carlton, Jim. "Picking Up Roots to Follow Ramtha." *The Orange County* [Calif.] *Register*, December 29, 1986.

Collins, Catherine, and Douglas Franz. "Let Us Prey." *Modern Maturity* 22 (June 1994): 22–32.

Crutcher, John. "Ramtha, the Enlightened One?" Parts 1 and 2. *Common Ground* 10 (July 1995): 24–27, 38–39; (August 1995): 21–25, 35.

Danese, Roseann. "A Match Made in Heaven." *The Windsor* [Ontario] *Star*, October 24, 1987.

Egan, Timothy. "Worldly and the Spiritual Clash in New Age Divorce." *The New York Times*, September 25, 1992.

French, Thomas. "Ramtha: Ancient Teacher or Fraud?" *St. Petersburg* [Fla.] *Times*, February 16, 1987.

Goldsmith, Steven. "Comings and Goings at Ranch Stir Town's Fears." *Seattle Post-Intelligencer*, October 12, 1989.

Hackett, George, with Pamela Abramson. "Ramtha, a Voice from Beyond." *Newsweek*, December 15, 1986.

Harrell, Ken. "Psychic Ordered Linda Evans to Rub Her Face in Horse Dung—And She Did." *Globe*, July 14, 1992.

Holland, Judy. "Dealing with Cults Can Be Dangerous to Your Health, Group Warns." [Olympia, Wash.] *The Olympian*, November 1, 1987.

Horne, Vance. "Pink Prophet? Woman Claims 35,000-Year-Old Spokesman for God Occupies Her Body." *Wausau* [Wis.] *Daily Herald*, August 21, 1986.

———. "Retailing Ramtha in Rainier." [Olympia, Wash.] *The Olympian*, May 28, 1986.

Ingle, Schuler. "Here's Ramtha!" *New Age Journal*, June 1986, 12.

Iwasaki, John. "JZ Knight Not Faking It, Say Scholars." *Seattle Post-Intelligencer*, February 10, 1997.

"JZ Knight/Ramtha in Sydney, 7/8th November 1987," *Australia's New Age News* 1, no. 10 (December 1987): 1, 20.

"J. Z. Knight Sued Over Horse Deal." *The Seattle Times*, October 11, 1989.

Kuechle, Jeff. "Designs on Ramtha." *The* [Portland] *Oregonian*, January 16, 1987.

Lattin, Don. "Northwest Drawing Doomsayers." *San Francisco Chronicle*, September 4, 1989.

"Linda Evans Wedding Plans Hit a Snag over New Age Guru's Role in Ceremony." *Star*, September 7, 1993.

Lindsey, Robert. "Teachings of 'Ramtha' Draws Hundreds West." *The New York Times*, November 16, 1986.

Lowry, Katherine. "Channelers." *Omni* 10 (March 1988): 46–50, 146–50.

Marshall, John. "A Big Divorce in Yelm: Is This the Right Channel?" *Seattle Post-Intelligencer*, March 9, 1989.

———. "Threats Run Ramtha Out of Colorado." [Loveland, Colo.] *Daily Reporter Herald*, March 16, 1989.

Matassa, Mark. "New Age Is Fast Becoming Old Hat in Yelm—Small Town Learns to Live with 'Ramtha.'" *The Seattle Times*, April 17, 1990.

Melton, J. Gordon. "An Initial Encounter with Ramtha." *Gnosis* (Fall 1996): 13–18.

Modie, Neil. "Yelm Medium Secure in Her Identity and Ramtha's." *Seattle Post-Intelligencer*, July 26, 1995.

"New Age Leader Rouses Town." [Salem, Ore.] *Statesman Journal*, October 10, 1989.

O'Toole, Kevin. "Ancient Spirit Speaks through Housewife." *Weekly World News*, May 24, 1983.

Pristin, Terry. "The Other Gurus Who Guide the Stars." *Los Angeles Times*, February 16, 1992.

Rhodes, Elizabeth. "State of Mind: JZ Knight Preaches Self-Love through a 35,000-Year-Old Spirit." *The Seattle Times*, October 25, 1987.

Ryon, Ruth. "Linda Evans Seeks Role as Landlady." *Los Angeles Times*, August 27, 1989.

Satir, F. E. "JZ Knight's Journey Began Years Ago." [Olympia, Wash.] *The Olympian*, February 16, 1997.

———. "Ramtha's School's First Test." *The Olympian*, February 16, 1997.

———. "Shining Light on Ramtha." *The Olympian*, February 6, 1997.

"Some in Yelm Hoping to Tune Out New Age Channeler." *The [Portland] Oregonian*, October 10, 1989.

Vrazo, Fawn. "Indeed!" *Albuquerque Journal Magazine* (May 31, 1983): 12, 14–15. First published as "By a Spirit Possessed: An Ancient Voice Lures a Modern Audience." *The Philadelphia Inquirer*, April 7, 1983.

Williams, B. J. "Head Trip." *Northwest Magazine*, August 9, 1987, 7–10.

Zohs, Christina. "In Search of the Self: The Role of Consciousness in the Construction of Reality." *The Golden Thread*, March 1997, 9–16.

RELATED MATERIALS

Books

Allen, Paul Marshall, comp. *A Christian Rosenkreutz Anthology*. Blauvelt, N.Y.: Rudolf Steiner Publications, 1968. Reprint, 2nd ed., vol. 10 of Spiritual Science Library, Blauvelt, N.Y.: Garber Communications, 1981.

Andrae, Valentin [Christian Rosencreutz, pseud.]. *Fama Fraternitatis (1614); Confessio Fraternitatis (1615); Chymische Hochzeit: Christiani Rosencreutz, Anno 1459 (1616)*. Edited by Richard van Dülmen. 3rd ed. Stuttgart: Calwer, 1981.

Bailey, Alice A. *Discipleship in the New Age*. Philadelphia: George S. Ferguson, 1944. Reprint, 1976.

———. *A Treatise on Cosmic Fire*. New York: Lucis Publishing, 1925. Reprint, 1995.

———. *A Treatise on White Magic*. New York: Lucis Publishing, 1934. Reprint 1991.

Bjorling, Joel. *Channeling: A Bibliographic Exploration*. New York: Garland Publishing, 1992.

Blavatsky, Helena Petrovna. *The Secret Doctrine*. 2 vols. London: London Theosophical House, 1889. Reprint, Pasadena, Calif.: Theosophical University Press, 1988.

Bloom, William, ed. *The New Age: An Anthology of Essential Writings*. London: Rider, 1991.

Bro, Harmon Hartzell. *A Seer Out of Season: The Life of Edgar Cayce*. New York: New American Library, 1989.

209

Buck, J. D. *Mystic Masonry*. Cincinnati, Ohio: Robert Clarke Co., 1887. Reprint, Kila, Mont.: Kessinger, 1994.

Cayce, Hugh Lynn. *Earth Changes Update*. Virginia Beach, Va.: ARE Press, 1980.

Cherry, Joanna. *Ascension for You and Me*. Mt. Shasta, Calif.: Ascension Mastery International, 1985.

Clark, Elmer Talmage. *The Psychology of Religious Awakening*. New York: Macmillan, 1929. Reprint, Ann Arbor, Mich.: University Microfilms International, 1980.

——. *The Small Sects in America*. Nashville: Cokesbury, 1937. Rev. ed., Nashville: Abingdon, 1965.

Clawson, Mary Ann. *Constructing Brotherhood: Class, Gender, and Fraternalism*. Princeton, N.J.: Princeton University Press, 1989.

David-Neel, Alexandria. *Magic and Mystery in Tibet*. New York: University Books, 1965.

de Montfaucon de Villars, Abbé N. *Comte de Gabalis: Discourses on the Secret Sciences and Mysteries in Accordance with the Principles of the Ancient Magi and the Wisdom of the Kabalistic Philosophers*. Kila, Mont.: Kessinger, 1992.

Deveney, John Patrick. *Paschal Beverly Randolph: A Nineteenth-Century Black American Spiritualist, Rosicrucian, and Sex Magician*. Albany: State University of New York Press, 1997.

Don, Frank. *Earth Changes Ahead*. New York: Warner, 1981.

Dean, Douglas, et al. *Executive ESP*. Englewood Cliffs, N.J.: Prentice-Hall, 1974.

Dowling, Levi H. *The Aquarian Gospel of Jesus the Christ*. 1907. Reprint, Marina del Rey, Calif.: DeVorss, 1991.

Faivre, Antoine, and Jacob Needleman, eds. *Modern Esoteric Spirituality*. New York: Crossroad, 1992.

Fillmore, Charles. *Prosperity*. Kansas City, Mo.: Unity School of Christianity, 1936. Reprint, Lee's Summit, Mo.: Unity, 1979.

Fisher, Joe. *Hungry Ghosts: An Investigation into Channeling and the Spirit World*. Toronto: McClelland & Stewart, 1990.

Fludd, Robert. *A Compendius Apology for the Fraternity of the Rosy Cross*. Leyden, The Netherlands: Godfrey Basson, 1616.

Godwin, Joscelyn. *The Theosophical Enlightenment*. Albany: State University of New York Press, 1994.

Goodman, Jeffrey. *We Are the Earthquake Generation*. New York: Seaview, 1978.

Grant, Robert M. *Gnosticism: A Source Book of Heretical Writings from the Early Christian Period*. New York: Harper & Brothers, 1961.

Great Cosmic Being Beloved Mighty Victory (Spirit). *The "I AM" Discourses*. The Saint Germain Series, vol. III. Channeled by Guy Warren Ballard. Chicago: Saint Germain Press, 1935. Reprint, Schaumberg, Ill.: Saint Germain Press, 1993.

Hastings, Arthur. *With the Tongues of Men and Angels: A Study of Channeling*. Fort Worth, Tex.: Holt, Rinehart & Winston, 1991.

Heelas, Paul. *The New Age Movement*. Oxford: Blackwell Publishers, 1996.

Holmes, Ernest. *The Science of Mind*. New York: Robert M. McBride and Co., 1926.

Jinarajadasa, Curuppumullage. *The Early Teachings of the Masters, 1881–1883*. Adyar, Madras, India: Theosophical Publishing House, 1923.

———. *Letters from the Masters of Wisdom*. 2 vols. Adyar, Madras, India: Theosophical Publishing House, 1919, 1925. Reprint, Wheaton, Ill.: Theosophical Publishing House, 1988.

Judith, Anodea. *Wheels of Life: A User's Guide to the Chakra System*. St. Paul, Minn.: Llewellyn Publications, 1986.

Kautz, William, and Melanie Brannon. *Channeling: The Intuitive Connection*. San Francisco: Harper & Row, 1987.

Klimo, Jon. *Channeling: Investigations on Receiving Information from Paranormal Sources*. Los Angeles: Jeremy P. Tarcher, 1987.

Krishna, Gopi. *The Biological Basis of Religion and Genius*. New York: Harper & Row, 1972.

Kyle, Richard. *The New Age Movement in American Culture*. Lanham, Md.: University Press of America, 1995.

Landsdowne, Zachery F. *The Chakras and Esoteric Healing*. Weir's Beach, Maine: Samuel Weiser, 1986.

Leadbeater, Charles Webster. *The Chakras*. Adyar, Madras, India: Theosophical Publishing House, 1927. Reprint, Wheaton, Ill.: Theosophical Publishing House, 1990.

———. *The Masters and the Path*. Adyar, Madras, India: Theosophical Publishing House, 1927. 4th ed., abridged, 1983.

211

———. *A Textbook of Theosophy*. Adyar, Madras, India: Theosophical Publishing House, 1912. Reprint, 1979.

Levison, Daniel J. *The Seasons of a Man's Life*. New York: Alfred A. Knopf, 1978.

Lewis, James R., and J. Gordon Melton, eds. *Perspectives on the New Age*. Albany: State University of New York Press, 1992.

Livtag, Irving. *Singer in the Shadows: The Strange Case of Patience Worth*. New York: Macmillan, 1972.

Lynn, Steven Jay, and Judith W. Rhue, eds. *Dissociation: Clinical and Theoretical Perspectives*. New York: Guilford Publications, 1994.

MacLaine, Shirley. *Dancing in the Light*. New York: Bantam Books, 1985.

———. *Out on a Limb*. New York: Ballantine, 1983.

Marrs, Texe. *Dark Secrets of the New Age*. Westchester, Ill.: Crossways Books, 1987.

———. *Mystery Mark of the New Age*. Westchester, Ill.: Crossways Books, 1988.

McIntosh, Christopher. *The Rosy Cross Unveiled*. Wellingborough, Northamptonshire, U.K.: Aquarian Press, 1980.

Melton, J. Gordon. *Encyclopedia of American Religions*. 5th ed. Detroit: Gale Research Co., 1996.

———. *Encyclopedia of Occultism and Parapsychology*. 4th ed. 2 vols. Detroit: Gale Research Co., 1996.

———. "Paschal Beverly Randolph: America's Pioneer Occultist." In Jean-Baptiste Martin and Francoise LaPlantine, ed., *Le Defi Magique: Esoterisme, Occultisme, Spiritisme*. Lyon, France: Presses Universitair de Lyon, 1994.

———, Jerome Clark, and Aidan Kelly, eds. *New Age Encyclopedia*. Detroit: Gale Research Co., 1990; *New Age Almanac*. Detroit: Visible Ink Press, 1990.

———, and George M. Eberhart. *The Flying Saucer Contactee Movement: 1950–1990*. Santa Barbara, Calif.: Santa Barbara Centre for Humanistic Studies, 1990.

———, and Robert L. Moore. *The Cult Experience: Responding to the New Religious Pluralism*. New York: Pilgrim Press, 1982.

Montgomery, Ruth. *Aliens Among Us*. New York: Putnam's, 1985.

Moody, Raymond. *Life After Life*. New York: Bantam Books, 1975.

Newbrough, John Ballou. *Oahspe: A New Bible in the Words of Jehovih and His Angel Embassadors; A Sacred History of the Dominions of the Higher and Lower Heavens on the Earth for the Past Twenty-four Thousand Years . . . .* New York: Oahspe Publishing Association, 1882. Reprint, Amherst, Wis.: Palmer, 1972.

Ornstein, Robert. *Multimind*. Boston: Houghton-Mifflin, 1986.

Osis, Karlis, and Eriendur Haraldsson. *At the Hour of Death*. New York: Hastings House, 1986.

Perkins, Lynn F. *The Masters As New Age Mentors*. Lakemont, Ga.: CSA Press, 1976.

Phillips, J. B. *Ring of Truth: A Translator's Testimony*. New York: Macmillan, 1967.

Pike, Albert. *Morals and Dogma of the Ancient and Accepted Scottish Rite of Freemasonry*. Richmond, Va.: L. H. Jenkins, 1871. Reprint, Kila, Mont.: Kessinger, 1992.

Ponder, Catherine. *The Dynamic Laws of Prosperity*. Englewood Cliffs, N.J.: Prentice-Hall, 1962.

Prince, Walter Franklin. *The Case of Patience Worth*. Boston: Boston Society for Psychical Research, 1927. Reprint, New Hyde Park, N.Y.: University Books, 1964.

Prophet, Elizabeth Clare. *The Great White Brotherhood in the History, Culture, and Religion of America*. Los Angeles: Summit University Press, 1976.

Raschke, Carl A. *The Interruption of Eternity: Modern Gnosticism and the True Origins of the New Religious Consciousness*. Chicago: Nelson-Hall, 1980.

——. *Painted Black: From Drug Killings to Heavy Metal: The Alarming True Story of How Satanism Is Terrifying Our Communities*. San Francisco: Harper & Row, 1990.

Rendel, Peter. *Introduction to the Chakras*. London: Aquarian Press, 1979.

Roberts, Allen E. *Freemasonry in American History*. Richmond, Va.: Macoy Publishing & Masonic Supply Co., 1985.

Roberts, Jane. *How to Develop Your ESP Power*. New York: F. Fell, 1966. Reprint, Hollywood, Fla.: Lifetime, 1997.

Roman, Sanaya, and Duane Packer. *Creating Money*. Tiburon, Calif.: HJ Kramer, 1988.

Sachse, Julius Friedrich. *The German Pietists of Provincial Pennsylvania, 1694–1708*. Philadelphia, 1895. Reprint, New York: AMS Press, 1970.

Scott-Elliott, William. *The Story of Atlantis, and, The Lost Lemuria*. London: Theosophical Publishing House, 1925. Reprint, Wheaton, Ill.: Theosophical Press, 1962.

Segrue, Thomas. *There Is a River: The Story of Edgar Cayce*. New York: Henry Holt, 1945. Reprint, Alexandria, Va.: Time-Life, 1992.

Sharp, Elizabeth Amelia. *William Sharp (Fiona Macleod): A Memoir*. New York: Duffield & Co., 1910.

Sharp, William [Fiona Macleod, pseud.]. *The Divine Adventure*. Portland, Maine: T. B. Mosher, 1903.

——. *The Immortal Hour*. Portland, Maine: T. B. Mosher, 1907.

——. *The Sin-Eater*. Chicago: Stone & Kimball, 1895. Reprint, Freeport, N.Y.: Books for Libraries Press, 1971.

Simmons, Emogene S. *Introductory Study Course in Theosophy*. 2 vols. Wheaton, Ill.: Department of Education, Theosophical Society in America, 1935. Revised edition, 1969.

Sinclair, John R. *The Alice Bailey Inheritance*. Wellingborough, Northamptonshire, U.K.: Turnstone Press, 1984.

Spraggett, Allen. *Arthur Ford, the Man Who Talked with the Dead*. New York: New American Library, 1973.

Stern, Jess. *Soul Mates*. New York: Bantam Books, 1984.

Stone, Joshua David. *The Complete Ascension Manual for the Aquarian Age*. Sedona, Ariz.: Light Technology Communication Services, 1994.

Stubbs, Tony. *An Ascension Handbook*. Livermore, Calif.: Oughton House Publications, 1991.

Theosophical Society. *A Primer of Theosophy: A Very Condensed Outline*. Chicago: Rajput Press, 1909.

Toth, Max, and Gary Nielsen. *Pyramid Power*. London: Freeway, 1974.

Troward, Thomas. *The Edinburgh Lectures on Mental Science*. New York: Robert M. McBride & Co., 1909. Reprint, Dodd, Mead, 1977.

Washington, Peter. *Madame Blavatsky's Baboon: A History of the Mystics, Mediums, and Misfits Who Brought Spiritualism to America*. New York: Schocken Books, 1995.

Weisberger, Richard William. *Speculative Freemasonry and the Enlightenment*. Boulder, Colo.: East European Monographs, 1993.

Wells, Roy A. *The Rise and Development of Organized Freemasonry*. London: Lewis Masonic, 1986.

Westen, Robin. *Channelers: A New Age Directory.* New York: Perigee Books, 1988.

Articles

Basu, B. D. "The Hindu System of Medicine." *Guy's Hospital Gazette* (London), 1889.

Introvigne, Massimo. "The Devil-Makers: Contemporary Evangelical Anti-Mormonism," *Dialogue: A Journal of Mormon Thought* 27, no. 1 (spring 1994): 153–69.

Montandon, Henri E. "Psychophysiological Aspects of the Kirlian Phenomenon: A Confirmatory Study." *Journal of the American Society for Psychical Research* 71, no. 1 (January 1977): 45–49.

Tinnin, L. "Mental Unity, Altered States of Consciousness, and Dissociation." *Dissociation* 3 (1990): 154–59.

ANCIENT GNOSTICISM (APPENDIX)

Abraham ben Simeon. *The Book of the Sacred Magic of Abra-Melin the Mage, As Delivered by Abraham the Jew unto His Son Lamech, A.D. 1458.* Translated by Samuel Liddell MacGregor Mathers. London: J. M. Watkins, 1898. Reprint, New York: Causeway, 1974.

Albertus, Frater. *The Alchemist of the Rocky Mountains.* Salt Lake City: Paracelsus Research Society, 1976.

Barbault, Armand. *Gold of a Thousand Mornings.* London: Neville Spearman, 1975.

Coudert, Allison. *Alchemy: The Philosopher's Stone.* London: Wildwood House, 1980.

Eliade, Mircea. *The Forge and the Crucible.* London: Rider, 1962.

de Givry, Grillot, trans. *A Pictorial Anthology of Witchcraft, Magic and Alchemy.* New Hyde Park, N.Y.: University Books, 1958.

Faivre, Antoine. *Access to Western Esotericism.* Albany: State University of New York Press, 1994.

———. *The Golden Fleece and Alchemy.* Albany: State University of New York Press, 1993.

Grabel, Kendrick, ed. *The Gospel of Truth.* Nashville, Tenn: Abingdon, 1960.

215

Grant, Robert M. *Gnosticism: A Source Book of Heretical Writings from the Early Christian Period.* New York: Harper & Brothers, 1961.

Hedrick, Charles W., and Robert Hodgson, Jr., eds. *Nag Hammadi, Gnosticism, and Early Christianity.* Peabody, Mass.: Hendrickson, 1986.

Hennecke, Edgar, ed. *New Testament Apocrypha. Vol. 1, Gospels and Related Writings.* Philadelphia: Westminster Press, 1963.

Trismegistus, Hermes. *Hermetica: The Ancient Greek and Latin Writings Which Contain Religious or Philosophical Teachings Ascribed to Hermes Trismegistus.* Translated by Walter Scott. Oxford: Clarendon, 1911. Reprint, Bath, England: Solos Press; Lower Lake, Calif.: Atrium, 1993.

——. *Thrice-Greatest Hermes; Studies in Hellenistic Theosophy and Gnosis.* Translated by George Robert Stow Mead. London: Theosophical Publishing Society, 1906. Reprint, Kila, Mont.: Kessinger, 1995.

Irenaeus. *Irenaeus of Lyons versus Contemporary Gnosticism: A Selection from Books I and II of Adversus Haereses.* Edited by Jan Tjeerd Nielsen. Leiden: E. J. Brill, 1977.

Jonas, Hans. *The Gnostic Religion: The Message of the Alien God and the Beginnings of Christianity.* Boston: Beacon Press, 1963.

Loos, Milan. *Dualistic Heresy in the Middle Ages.* Prague (Praha): Academia, 1974.

Regardie, Israel. *The Garden of Pomegranates.* London: Rider, 1932. Reprint: St. Paul, Minn.: Llewellyn Publications, 1970.

——. *The Middle Pillar: A Co-relation of the Principles of Analytical Psychology and the Elementary Techniques of Magic.* Chicago: Aries Press, 1933. Rev. ed., St. Paul, Minn.: Llewellyn Publications, 1970.

Reyner, J. H. *The Diary of a Modern Alchemist.* London: Neville Spearman, 1974.

Rudolph, Kurt. *Gnosis: The Nature and History of Gnosticism.* San Francisco: HarperSanFrancisco, 1987.

Widengren, George. *Mani and Manichaeism.* London: Weidenfelds & Nicholson, 1965.

216

Printed in the United States
By Bookmasters